Provence
HARVEST

WITH 40 RECIPES BY AWARD-WINNING CHEF *Jacques Chibois*

Text copyright © 2004 by Aubanel, une marque des editions Minerva, Geneve (Suisse)

Published in 2005 by
Stewart, Tabori & Chang
115 West 18th Street
New York, NY 10011
www.abramsbooks.com

Library of Congress Cataloging-in-Publication Data is on file with the Library of Congress.
ISBN: 1-58479-434-8

Translated by Louisa Jones

Recipes and Advice translated by Stephanie Curtis

The text of this book was composed in Bickley Script, Granjon, and Sabon.

Printed in China

10 9 8 7 6 5 4 3 2 1

First Printing

Stewart, Tabori & Chang is a subsidiary of

LA MARTINIÈRE

LOUISA JONES

Provence HARVEST

FOREWORD BY
DAN BARBER

PHOTOGRAPHS BY
GUY HERVAIS

WITH 40 RECIPES BY AWARD-WINNING CHEF *Jacques Chibois*

STEWART, TABORI & CHANG

NEW YORK

Foreword by Dan Barber
Introduction by Louisa Jones

CONTENTS

FOREWORD

I'VE NEVER MET JACQUES CHIBOIS, but I feel like I know him. I know how he must feel standing in the farmer's market come August. Thirteen years ago, I was there myself, facing a mountain of intoxicating apricots, a portly lady farmer bellowing at me irritably, as if to say, "Look here, you silly American, this is the essence of Provence. It will be gone soon and you'll be sorry. Mon Dieu, consume."

Homesick and exhausted, having logged six days a week for two hot months in a kitchen from 7AM to midnight, I knew strikingly little about Provence but didn't care, having decided to end my "stage" early and return home. I spent my last day walking around the farmer's market, and that's when I came upon the apricots and Madame farmer.

The fruit was like nothing I had ever seen: plump to nearly bursting, blushed a deep red.

"Apricot?" I asked, to be sure.

"Monsieur, des abricots," she said, pointing to the large sign.

I started to pick one out, but the Madame flicked my hand, and feeble attempt at identifying ripe fruits, aside. She played her fingers lovingly over her small treasures, landing on one with her middle finger and tapping it gently. "Parfait," she said, not to me, but to the apricot, holding the newborn up in the morning light. She wrapped it unhurriedly in beautiful tissue paper, ignoring my protests of wanting to eat it right away before handing it to me, almost reluctantly.

I took a bite. I cannot say what happened next. I was at once entranced and confused, not because I was tasting the best apricot of my life, but because I was tasting an apricot I had never imagined could exist.

In that moment of sheer bliss, gripping the apricot close to my mouth, I attempted in my best French to inquire about this tiny miracle: "C'etait ne, ou?" (This was born, where?). Without warning, my eyes teared up. I had to look away. It was the emotion of the moment—my two months in France were over, I was returning home to an unknown future—as much as it was the taste of the fruit.

Madame farmer turned red herself. She walked around her stall and put her arm around me. I spent the next half hour learning how to grow perfect apricots, about the importance of pruning, of climate, about the seed that had been with her family for two generations. I purchased an entire case.

More than a decade later, this wonderful book by Louisa Jones brings me right back to that Sunday afternoon at the market with my apricots. Louisa not only understands like few others the irrefutable link between the garden and our food, but she also somehow makes you feel that you are in the garden, smelling the basil, tasting the tomatoes, and hurrying along to make the gazpacho before the guests arrive.

Jones and Chibois have a big vision that's actually very small. Three-thousand miles across the Atlantic, I long for it. More has changed in our American food system in the last fifty years—in how food is grown, who's growing it, and how it's getting to you—than in the preceding 500, and the effects of those changes are only recently becoming clear—effects on our health, our environment, and the taste of our food. We have allowed (and as eaters, we have encouraged) economies of scale and the reductionism of marketing to do great damage to local agriculture, the family farm, and the quality and variety of foods available to us. Thousands of unique varieties of fruits, vegetables, grains, and livestock have been driven to near-extinction by a system that values appearance over flavor, portability over freshness, uniformity over diversity, and price over everything.

These changes have also had far-reaching effects on our communities. Agriculture produces not only commodities, but also livelihoods, cultures, and ecological services. One cannot distinguish between, say, what we feed our children for dinner and whether or not that square foot of planet earth will remain in pasture or succumb to suburban lawn. Everything is connected.

Therein lies *Provence Harvest*'s theme: all regional cuisines comprise a narrative. Historical background, customs, crafts, gardening, and, of course, food are all a part of the harvest, and they're interwoven into a fabric that makes it impossible to distinguish between the garden and the meal we share in it.

So why did that apricot taste so good? I'd argue it had as much to do with the care and pride the Madame took in picking it for me, or the beautiful Provençal paper she wrapped around it, as it did its ripeness.

Americans are obsessed with the Provençal way of life in part, I think, because Provence tells a story that Americans increasingly have trouble telling. It's a story that invites us to re-engage through a kind of ecological experience, an experience that includes not just the right produce picked at the perfect moment, but the relationships and history that give texture to that experience. One becomes a better-informed eater, all in the context of delight. What an enjoyable way to be in the world.

Dan Barber

INTRODUCTION

I first met Jacques Chibois in 1991 when he was still chef at the Royal Gray Hotel in Cannes. It was there, in the city, that he first earned his reputation for sensitive, simple-but-sophisticated cookery. Already a prizewinner many times over, in those days he was longing for a quiet country place of his own. What he later found is a treasure: the Bastide Saint Antoine in Grasse, an eighteenth century manor house with an old-fashioned terraced garden. Such properties are extremely rare in this region so sought after by the rich and famous. This one has now become the workshop of a great cook.

People often ask me, even in France, Why eat in an acclaimed but expensive restaurant when you can enjoy food prepared among friends or at the corner bistro? Jacques Chibois grew up with the best home cooking—his first teacher was his mother at her bistro in Limoges. But great chefs are like top fashion designers: They spare no expense to seek out the best possible raw materials which they then transform into rare creations. Their food is a form of fine art, an unforgettable voyage of discovery. I do not spend a lot of time following the starred restaurant circuit. My husband and I live quietly in the country where we have been growing our own vegetables for some thirty years. Many of our neighbors are farmers and vintners. My writing takes me to gardens, often food-producing, rather than restaurants. I admire Jacques Chibois's respect for both gardening and farming, his intimate knowledge of where food comes from and what happens to it along the way. For instance, he tells this story about growing up in the Limousin countryside: "When I was a kid, we had a piece of land right next to the neighbors', but sloping in a different direction. Both families grew potatoes, but my family sold ours and bought the neighbors' instead. Theirs had better flavor. Even though the two fields were only yards apart, the difference was appreciable." This is a gardener's tale as well as a cook's.

In this book, we pay homage together to a region which still cherishes such differences. This is not nostalgia. The countryside we see today is capable of adapting to new conditions, reinventing itself, renewing its resources in a context that is more and more "global."

Culinary history proves, if need be, that globalization began in the Stone Age. Provence has always been a crossroads for international exchange. Its famous Indian fabrics, vegetables like tomatoes and eggplant, and the codfish so essential to its rural cuisine are all age-old imports that contribute so much to the harvest we still enjoy today.

In some situations, globalization creates standardization. There are French farmers who now work under contract with huge companies that sow spinach or beans in all of the fields on a single day, harvesting everything with huge machines a few months later (again within twenty-four hours), regardless of variations in ripeness, soil or micro-climate. Such a farmer has just rented out his land; his intimate, individual experience of the soil's life and habits count for nothing. The vegetables thus grown give the consumer dubious quality, flavor, or even nutrition. In this book, we have tried to present growers, gardeners, and small-scale processors who resist the pressures of standardization. Some are involved in desperate struggles for survival—the Olivades farm near Toulon, for example (see Address list). Helping them is a gauge for the future of all of us.

English writer John Berger once wrote, "The world is leaving the earth behind." Jacques Chibois and I want to keep that from happening, as much as we can, in our own small corner. But this does not mean shutting out the world—far from it. We can, we must, join up with others all over the planet who want, as we do, to preserve local flavor and character. The Mediterranean region already offers great diversity, as do those parts of the world with similar climates like California, Australia, New Zealand, South Africa, South America, and China. Mediterranean tradition has, since Roman times, united beauty with productivity and elegance with earthiness. But this quiet enjoyment in everyday living can be experienced by people in every climate and country. The way of life we present in this book includes house and garden, fields and orchards. Daily health and well-being are one aspect, creative exploration is another. The past is important because it feeds the future. This is a book about harvest, abundance and variety —a cornucopia of flavors, traditions, cultures, exchanges, inventions, and discoveries all to come.

Louisa Jones

A House in Provence

«It is an old house, with sunny walls, ocher-toned like the earth. . . . It has a broad terrace carefully protected from the fierce mistral wind, where a pretty fountain spills into a pool.»

Jacqueline de Romilly

WHAT EXACTLY IS A *BASTIDE*?

*Above right:
Majestic trees, an
elegant fountain, a
symmetrical façade,
all signs of aristocratic
style, here at the
Pavillon de Galon.*

THE WORD *BASTIDE* EVOKES A COUNTRY HOUSE IN PROVENCE.
This word is a commercial siren song in Provence today, but what does it really mean? Thirteenth century manuscripts used it to describe fortifications, but by the seventeenth and eighteenth centuries, it had come to mean an elegant estate. Specialist Nerte Dautier compares the Provençal *bastide* to the Tuscan villa, both being "a kind of rural habitat which combines an aristocratic or middle-class residence with a working farm and gardens." She adds that "the *bastide* was a sound and lucrative investment, a country home and a place for leisure and repose. By the luxury of its appointments and the charm of its gardens, it betokened membership in the class privileged by Fortune." She lists hundreds of examples surrounding the city of Aix-en-Provence where Parliament met, seat also of the law courts and tax authorities until the French Revolution of 1789. Owners here first imitated foreign fashions—primarily Italian and Parisian—before evolving a style of their own. In the nineteenth century, bastides clustered mainly around the thriving port of Marseille. Émile Garcin, a real estate agent who specializes in this type of property, explains that owners of prestigious urban townhouses always had country *bastides* as well.

In Provence then, as in Italy, every city had a peppering of stately homes outside town, summer retreats whose owners escaped the heat of town while supervising the farming. Their elegant living was largely financed by the harvest. In Grasse, however, families owed their fortunes largely to the perfume industry. As the city expanded, the medieval stronghold was surrounded by a ring of *bastides*, each named for a saint. The Bastide Saint Antoine is now the home of Jacques Chibois.

Country estates in Provence remained modest compared to Loire Valley châteaus, built for kings, their families, and followers. The southern version is much smaller, in part due to laws that distributed wealth among heirs rather than giving all to the eldest son. But

southern homes were also retreats for private pleasures, not ostentatious statements of power. In the seventeenth century, the French minister Colbert reported bitterly to his king, "These degenerates in the vile holes they call stately homes in this country would rather give up the best deal in the world than miss some entertainment at the bastide." The nineteenth century novelist Balzac, who was from Touraine, was equally scornful. "A bastide: Four walls of pebbles held together by a yellowish sort of cement, covered with a roof of hollow red tiles, and sinking under the weight of all that brickwork!" he wrote. Today, however, northerners are buying up *bastides* at a great rate.

The word *mas* also designates country houses in parts of Provence. Originally this was the working farm attached to an estate or independent. There is some overlap between the terms *mas* and *bastide*. Provençal gentry never separated beauty and productivity, so orchards and vineyards spread around their homes like vast parterres. At the same time, an independent farmer of humble origin might himself become quite wealthy. Frédéric Mistral, a Provençal poet who won the Nobel Prize in 1904, described his father as belonging to this sort of peasant aristocracy. "The old bastide where I was born was called the *Mas du Juge*," he says.

Nonetheless, there are important distinctions. A *mas* is built near a spring, usually in a hollow, while the *bastide* sits on a rise from which it can command the countryside. Its owners can afford to have water piped in if necessary. The *mas* usually is made of rough-hewn stone, whereas the *bastide* covers these with a kind of cement and lime wash,

Above:
A bathroom, glimpsed from the balcony of the Villa Saint Louis.

Right:
A mas transformed into a bastide by the Lafourcade family.

either rose-, golden-, or ocher-toned. The *bastide* is generally square or rectangular and has a second story. Its windows are placed symmetrically around a central entrance that often opens under a wrought-iron balcony. In front of the *bastide* stretches a long esplanade matching the proportions of the façade, embellished with large, glazed Anduze pots and a fountain, and shaded by majestic plane trees. A *mas* usually has a broad trellis decked with a mix of vine and wisteria attached to its south wall to protect the entrance and provide summer shade. There is no statuary or parterre here, but usually clipped broadleaf laurel or laurustinus hedging that also acts as a windbreak.

Of course there have always been infinite combinations, and today many newcomers to the region are actively transforming *mas* into *bastides*. "You need an experienced eye to avoid a tasteless mishmash," insists Bruno Lafourcade, a specialist in elegant restoration. Above all, he feels restorers need to master traditional skills in order to preserve the essential harmony of each place. Victor Papernak, an architecture historian, writes about vernacular construction in a way that just suits the *bastide* ideal. "Vernacular buildings are ecologically apt, that is they fit in well with local climate, flora, fauna, and ways of life. . . . They recede into the environment rather than serving as self-proclaiming design statements; they are human in scale. . . . They tend to blur the differences between the dwellings of the aristocracy and the gentry, the home-workshops of artisans, the homes of the very poor, farmhouses and barns." He attributes "sensuous frugality that results in true elegance" to vernacular structures all over the world. Provence has inherited this tradition, still very much alive today.

Roast partridge
with chestnuts and juniper berries

FOR 4 SERVINGS:

— FOR THE PARTRIDGE: 4 SMALL PARTRIDGES (WITH THEIR LIVERS), SALT, PEPPER, 1¼ OUNCES LARD OR FATBACK, 1½ TABLESPOONS UNSALTED BUTTER

— FOR THE JUS: 2 SHALLOTS, 1 CARROT, 1 SLICE (1¼ OUNCES) CELERY ROOT, 3 JUNIPER BERRIES, PINCH FRESH THYME, ½ BAY LEAF, 2 SPRIGS DRIED FENNEL, 4 SLICES DRIED CÈPE MUSHROOMS, ¼ CUP MARC DE PROVENCE*, ¼ CUP DRY WHITE WINE, 2 TEASPOONS UNSALTED BUTTER, ¼ CUP OLIVE OIL.

— FOR THE VEGETABLES: 2 FENNEL BULBS, 8 FLORETS CAULIFLOWER, 3½ OUNCES CHESTNUTS, 1½-2 TABLESPOONS UNSALTED BUTTER, SALT, PEPPER

— FOR THE PRESENTATION: 20 JUNIPER BERRIES, A FEW DROPS OLIVE OIL

The partridge

Preheat the oven to 400°F. Season the partridge, inside and out, with salt and pepper, and truss them. Cut the lard in cubes and melt in a Dutch oven over high heat. Place the partridge, breast side down, in the hot fat. When well browned, turn the birds on their backs, and bake, uncovered, in the hot oven for 10 minutes. Remove while they are still rare and let rest on a rack in the warm oven (turned off). When the partridge are cool enough to handle, separate the legs and the breasts from the carcasses, cover with aluminum foil, and set aside. Just before serving, reheat the partridge in the oven with the butter.

The jus*

Peel and chop the shallots, carrot, and celery root. Break up the partridge carcasses and brown them in the Dutch oven with the livers, shallots, carrot, and celery root. Add the juniper berries, fresh thyme, bay leaf, dried fennel, and dried cèpes. Flame with the marc de Provence or other brandy, add the white wine and ½ cup water. Cook for 35 minutes over a low heat. Strain the juices into a saucepan and let reduce over low heat. Whisk in the butter and olive oil.

The vegetables

Rinse the fennel bulbs and cut horizontally into ¼-inch slices. Remove the heart and any woody parts. Cook in a saucepan of boiling salted

water (1½ tablespoons salt for 1 quart water) for 7 minutes, then plunge
the fennel into cold water and drain immediately. Slice the cauliflower
florets into ⅛-inch slices. Season with salt and pepper, and brown in butter in a non-stick skillet, turning the slices, for 5 minutes. Combine the
fennel and the cauliflower. Preheat the oven to 350°F. Cut across at the
base of each chestnut and place on a baking sheet or in an iron skillet in
the oven for 20 minutes. Peel the chestnuts, remove the thin inner skin,
and cut into thin slices.

Presentation

Arrange a bed of fennel and cauliflower on each plate, top with the partridge. Spoon the sauce around and sprinkle with chestnuts. Arrange a
line of crushed juniper berries on the edge of each plate and finish with
a drizzle of olive oil.

* MARC DE PROVENCE *is a white brandy from Provence. subtitute any good quality*
brandy, preferably clear.

** A JUS *is a light sauce.*

CHEF'S NOTE

Choose gray partridge, if available.
These are game birds, and therefore
will be the freshest available.

The Chef's Advice

READING A RECIPE

When chefs cook, all of our senses are at work; first our taste buds and our eyes, of course, but also our sense of smell and even our ears. Our ears hear if something is cooking too quickly. All of this is difficult to explain in a cookbook, or to put in a recipe, and some readers have a better feeling for these intangibles than others. We chefs are often told: "You hide half of the recipe, you have your little secrets." My response to this is: "No and yes!" No, because we share our recipes with sincerity, without hiding anything. Yes, because there are certain instinctive things that cannot be expressed easily. Why is it that just hearing a dish simmer or sauté, we know that it is either not hot enough or too hot? Each piece of equipment is different (and makes a difference), as is each product. This is a little complicated: in French we call it a "tour de main," a certain know-how or a knack.

So, it is important to watch, smell, and taste at all times. Those who set out to reproduce a chef's recipe should be truly immersed: they should reread the recipe several times, study it and visualize the final results. Next, one should, perhaps, simply close the cookbook. When we begin to learn to cook, we too frequently tend to read recipes word for word, while the most important thing is to try to understand the whole, to fully grasp what we are going to do. Later, everyone can add his or her own little "tour de main," his own spin on a recipe, born from his own imagination. Michel Guérard used to explain to us every little detail of each recipe, and then at the end he would say: "Now it's up to you, figure it out for yourself."

Learning to cook means knowing how to read and to listen! But it also means not complicating recipes and knowing how to keep things simple.

BRUNCH IN PROVENCE

Olive trees—on the plate and in the garden.

Jacques Chibois likes to translate american-style brunch into the Provençal idiom—a hybrid sweet-and-savory meal for lazy, late weekend mornings when a family can relax together. "I picture it in a garden," he says, "with shade and sun, country murmurs and birdsong—all the surroundings that contribute to the comforts of a leisurely meal. Fruit and flowers just picked, hot pastries just out of the oven or brought home from a quick trip to the neighborhood bakery. The freshness of the food echoes the cool of a summer morning in Provence, before the heat of the day."

Such a brunch might mingle Anglo-Saxon breakfast traditions with the customs of Provence for a blending of fragrance and color, lightness and elegance. Of course, traditional farm breakfasts had to be substantial, heavy in fat, protein, and carbohydrates as a necessary preparation for a hard day's physical labor ahead. Sweets were never important in this menu, nor generally in the Provençal diet. In her book *Histoire des recettes provençales*, Simone Villevieille recounts that southerners have always preferred bitter, acidic, and salty flavors to sugary ones. Even in middle-class homes, children coming home from school were often given a slab of bread rubbed with olive oil and garlic, rather than cake or cookies. The famous "thirteen desserts" of the Christmas Eve supper includes various dried fruits and nuts and only one pastry, a cake made from bread dough enriched for the occasion with milk, eggs, and olive oil. Butter and cream, not generally available locally, became the privilege of an urban elite who could import them from elsewhere.

But if rich, sweet desserts are rare in Mediterranean cuisine, sweet and savory mixes, like those appreciated in American brunches, are another story. Parisian-based haute cuisine has avoided such combinations since the seventeenth century—just as classical French literature refused to mix tragedy and comedy. The cuisine of Provence, on the contrary, has

Fresh produce and the cool of a summer morning in the garden.

always welcomed them. The famous Nice *tourte* made of spinach or chard with raisins and pine nuts is very old but still much appreciated today and makes a wonderful brunch dish. Honey as well as fruit was used to sweeten certain mixtures, since Provençal farmers have been beekeepers since ancient times. Honey was originally used more for medicinal than culinary purposes, as it was thought to strengthen muscles, act as a natural antibiotic, and help in the healing of wounds and burns. Cane sugar was also first introduced in Provence as a medicine, known as "reed honey" as early as the sixteenth century because of the look of the plant. It remained rare and expensive until the late nineteenth century. One of the first to experiment in cooking with cane sugar was the good doctor Nostradamus, born in 1503 in Saint-Rémy-de-Provence. The tale is told that after some years of famine, where fresh fruit and vegetable harvests were lost because there was no means for preserving them, Nostradamus tried to find a solution using honey, grape must (residue after pressing the wine), and cane sugar. In 1555, he published, along with his famous book of prophecies, a treatise on jam-making.

Nostradamus imagined jams flavored with spices like ginger, cinnamon, cloves, and pepper. For those who could afford such luxury, jams were sometimes mixed with wine as a way of using up doubtful vintages! This alchemist-magician invented many other combinations with candied fruit, marmalades, and jellies, as well as pastes of quince, pears, plums, oranges, lemons, carrots, beets, and pumpkin. He developed a melon jam, a version of which is still commonly made today in Provence using a variety of a fruit called citre. Quince jam

was recommended as a face mask to improve the complexion.

Jacques Chibois might be considered a present-day alchemist, testing unusual blends. The sweet-and-savory contrasts he appreciates are not so much with sour tastes, more common in northern and eastern France, as with acidic ingredients. In the south, the hot summer sun concentrates the natural sugars of fruit and vegetables. Chibois feels a touch of acid, often in the form of local lemon juice, accentuates this flavor. Citrus is highly appropriate for brunches, where American-style orange juice remains a must. Sun-drenched tomatoes are also honored guests, chosen from among the 400 varieties currently available from seeds collected all over the world (see page 140).

Jacques Chibois also adds lemon and cinnamon to fig jam and serves it with honey-based pastry. Fruit also appears "just slightly jellified" as juice and as mixed salads perfumed with mint, basil, and bee-balm. Other baked goods served at brunch include the little braided pastries traditionally made in Grasse called *fougassettes*, a very old recipe, similar to the Christmas oil bread. Sometimes there are omelettes made from local farm eggs and tiny spring artichokes, his own homemade sausage and ham, fresh white cheese from the mountains above Grasse, and Gariguette strawberries.

*Above right:
A Provençal-American
brunch mixes sweet,
acidic, and salty
flavors.*

The new Provençal brunch offers a chance to experiment with unusual flavor blends. It mixes influences from the four corners of the earth with ancient traditions of the local *terroir*.

Summer melon
prepared simply with lemon grass

FOR 4 SERVINGS:
— FOR THE MELONS: 5 RIPE PROVENÇAL MELONS*, 4 TABLESPOONS FINELY CHOPPED LEMONGRASS, ⅔ CUP MUSCAT DE BEAUMES-DE-VENISE**
— FOR THE PRESENTATION: 4 LEAVES LEMONGRASS, A FEW WHITE FLOWERS SUCH AS JASMINE OR ALMOND BLOSSOMS

The melons

Cut the melons in half, and remove the rind and seeds. Cut 4 of the melons into even wedges and roll half of them (see photo) in the finely chopped lemongrass. Arrange the melon wedges in well-chilled shallow plates or bowls, alternating lemongrass-coated and plain slices. Process the remaining melon with the Muscat wine, reducing it to a smooth purée.

Presentation

Pour the melon sauce around the melon slices. Decorate each plate with lemongrass leaves and white flowers. Serve very cold.

* MELONS DE PROVENCE: *sweet little orange-fleshed summer melons from the Provence region. They can be replaced with cantaloupe or muskmelon.*

** BEAUMES-DE-VENISE: *a sweet, pale gold wine made in the village of Beaumes-de-Venise from the Muscat grape. Substitute other sweet Muscat wines.*

CHEF'S NOTE

The quality of the melon is essential: choose pretty little Provençal melons, perfectly ripened.

Warm french scrambled eggs
with mint, red berries and lavender sauce

For 4 servings:
— For the lavender sauce: ⅔ cup cream, ¼ cup granulated sugar, ½ teaspoon lavender flowers*, ½ teaspoon cornstarch
— For the scrambled eggs: 8 eggs, ¼ cup granulated sugar, 2 teaspoons unsalted butter, 1 tablespoon cream, 2 tablespoons finely chopped fresh mint
— For the presentation: 4½ ounces (about 1 cup) strawberries, 4½ ounces wild strawberries, 4½ ounces raspberries, 4½ ounces red currants, 4½ ounces blackberries, powdered sugar, a few lavender flowers or mint leaves

The lavender sauce

Bring the cream and the sugar to a boil in a saucepan. Remove from the heat, add the lavender flowers and let infuse for 1 minute, then strain immediately. Dissolve the cornstarch in 1 tablespoon water, add to the lavender cream, and bring to a boil stirring. Let cool and refrigerate covered.

The eggs

Whisk the eggs and sugar together. Melt the butter in a small sauté pan, add the eggs and cook over low heat, whisking constantly. When thickened, but still very creamy, add the cream and the mint.

Presentation

Pour the eggs in a neat round in the center of each serving plate, arrange the fruit on top and sprinkle with powdered sugar. Spoon a ribbon of lavender sauce around and decorate with lavender flowers or mint leaves.

* Lavender flowers: *use untreated lavender flowers (fresh or dried) being very careful not to let them infuse too long, or the sauce will be overpowering. In some cases, just a few seconds is enough to give the sauce a hint of lavender flavor.*

CHEF'S NOTE

Be sure not to overcook the eggs, and serve on warm plates.

HOUSEHOLD LINENS

Dor centuries, Provence was a crossroads between northern Europe and the Mediterranean world. In the Middle Ages, the Fair of Beaucaire on the lower Rhône river was one of the greatest on the continent, offering Flemish linens alongside cottons from Egypt and the Levant. Local materials were also used for household furnishings. According to Michel Biehn, a specialist in Provençal costumes and fabrics, people made sheets out of hemp and even nettles. This custom held until the nineteenth century, that golden age of country living in Provence still so often idealized today. Large family farmsteads prospered in those days, like the one where poet Frédéric Mistral spent his boyhood. In his memoirs, the writer described dividing up household goods after his father's death, listing all the local items that sell today as expensive antiques. "The contents of the house, the furniture, the big four-poster beds, the kneading trough with its iron fittings, the flour mill, the polished wardrobes, the carved bread bin, the table, the rack for glasses that I had seen fixed to those walls since my birth, the dozens of plates and flowered pottery that never left the shelves of the sideboard, the sheets of hemp that my mother had spun with her own hand . . ." (translation George Wickes, *The Memoirs of Frédéric Mistral,* New Directions 1985).

In those days, elegant townsfolk preferred immaculate linens embroidered according to the latest Parisian fashion, while peasant families like Mistral's kept to the tradition of rough-woven sheets with a long center seam. Michel Biehn comments that it is these coarser fabrics that are so very fashionable today. "Such sheets also took a long time to blanch. Linen turned white in only three washings, but hemp might take a hundred years to reach the same stage," he says. In farmsteads, a huge washing called the *bugada* took place only twice a year, spring and fall. Everything was soaked for a day and a night with washing soda crystals, then rinsed for the first

For Edith Mézard,
"the eye works in har-
mony with the hand."

time. On the second evening, a huge vat was set up on a tripod over an open fire and the washing was "poured" (that is, stacked between layers of ash and then subjected to repeated rinsing) all night long. Each household had large stocks of sheets. A housewife was judged on the state of her closets and cupboards. When she married, a young bride was given the keys to all, which confirmed that she had indeed become mistress of the household.

Marriages, like births, provided opportunity for the finest displays. The marriage bed must have a counterpoint in piped vermicelli quilting, a masterpiece of the young bride's trousseau. No doubt she was helped in making this by her mother and aunts, observes Michel Biehn, for the skills required to execute such work are considerable. But there were also embroidery workshops where expert professionals, usually cloistered nuns, produced exceptional results.

Curiously, woolen bedcovers were not common in Provence. Wool was certainly produced and processed, especially at L'Isle-sur-la-Sorgue, because sheep have been part of the Provençal landscape since Neolithic times. But bedcovers were largely made by inserting a thickness of woolen wadding between two sheets of cotton. These quilting techniques, as well as the most common motifs, were brought back by the Marseille traders from the far countries that lay along the great silk route. The first examples appear in Marseille as of the fourteenth century. Today, our expert explains, the word *boutis* has

become a general term meaning anything quilted. But in the true *boutis*, the stitching comes first and the stuffing afterwards—which requires patience and precision.

In the Luberon, Édith Mézard directs an embroidery workshop that maintains the quality and rigor of the craftswomen so highly appreciated in past centuries. For her, household linens are a very personal matter. "They are not a luxury, but something that breathes with the house. Each person has an individual style, according to his or her nature and needs," she says. In addition, Mézard admires "the magnificent art of the nuns" and observes that "what really distinguishes that ancient handicraft is the notion of time it involves. This is really crucial. You feel in this needlework that time is pleasure, and this is why the results are so beautiful. The woman who made this or that piece did it with love. I regard these antique fabrics as a gift from the past." She continues these traditions with her own team of skilled craftswomen. "We embroider for people who will take real pleasure in touching and looking. The pleasantest fabrics to work with have been the same since the beginnings of civilization: linen, silk, and, of course, cotton. This is craft and not art, insofar as the work is really repetitive. But the more practice your hand gets, the more skillful it becomes." She adds, "I am really lucky to be able to do something I love so much." Even daily upkeep seems to her an act of love, a gift. Ironing sheets for her three sons is like making their favorite chocolate cake or a gratin with the first pumpkin of the season.

Jacques Chibois appreciates all the traditional furnishings of his *bastide* in the same way. His ideal here as in the building itself is a mix of simplicity and elegance. He likes "soft fabrics, pleasant to the touch that have weight and volume. They may be arranged informally, but this disarray is not really untidy, it is harmonious, rounded, easy to live with, like the tiled floors. And the more things age, the more they take on a character of their very own."

Above:
The cupboards of
Michel Biehn display
the spoils of a great
collector.

Right:
A finely worked
petticoat at the
Costume and Jewelry
Museum of Grasse.

Pears roasted with spices

For 4 servings:
— For the pears in syrup: 2 pears, 1 cup mineral water, 6½ tablespoons granulated sugar, 1 vanilla bean, 2 pinches saffron threads, 1 cinnamon stick, 1 star anise, zests of 2 untreated lemons, a few drops lemon juice, 1½ tablespoons unsalted butter.
— For the pear compote: 5 pears, 1¼ tablespoons unsalted butter, 1½ tablespoons granulated sugar, ½ ounce (½ tablespoon) grated fresh ginger or 1 pinch powdered ginger
— For the cinnamon cream: 1 cup whipping cream, ½ vanilla bean, 1 tablespoon honey, 1 pinch ground cinnamon, zest of 1 untreated orange.
— For the sauce: 1 cup syrup from the pears, ½ teaspoon cornstarch, 1 tablespoon pear brandy
— For the presentation: whole spices such as star anise, cinnamon sticks, vanilla bean pods

Pears in syrup

Peel the pears. Bring the mineral water to a boil in a saucepan with ⅓ cup (5½ tablespoons) of the sugar. Split the vanilla bean in half lengthwise and add it to the saucepan along with the saffron, cinnamon, star anise, lemon zests, and juice.

Poach the pears in the syrup. Test for doneness with the tip of a paring knife, remove from the heat and let the pears cool in their syrup. When cool, drain the pears, reserving the syrup for the sauce. Halve the pears, removing cores and seeds. Brown them in a skillet with the butter and the remaining tablespoon sugar. Set aside at room temperature.

The pear compote

Peel the pears, cut them in half, remove the cores and seeds, and cut into cubes. Brown the pear cubes in a skillet with the butter and sugar. Add the grated fresh ginger.

The whipped cinnamon cream

Whip the cream to soft peaks in a large chilled bowl. Scrape the seeds from the vanilla bean and add to the whipped cream along with the honey, cinnamon, and orange zest. Refrigerate.

The sauce

Bring the reserved pear syrup to a boil in a saucepan. Dissolve the cornstarch in the pear brandy and add to the syrup. Warm over low heat for 5 minutes until thickened. Whisk until the sauce is smooth and let cool.

Presentation

Arrange a little of the pear compote on each plate using a 4-inch diameter pastry ring to make a neat circle. Using a pastry bag fitted with a plain tip, pipe a few rosettes of the cinnamon cream on each serving. Top each serving with a poached pear half and spoon the sauce around. Decorate the plates with the whole spices.

CHEF'S NOTE

Poach the pears a day in advance; they will absorb the flavors of the spices better. This dessert can be enriched with a scoop of vanilla or pineapple ice cream.

Conseil du chef

COOKING WITH HONEY

Above all, it is important to know that the less a honey has been tampered with or manipulated, the more taste it will have. For example, look for honeys that have not been heated. Here at the Bastide, we make many recipes with honey. Honey ice cream is fabulous, as are sauces made with honey. Fish served with a sauce made with honey is excellent, particularly when lemon is added. It's true that lemon adds a little "punch" or a counterpoint to the sweetness of honey, sometimes too cloying, and it releases incomparable flavors. Imagine a duck with honey mixed with spices, such as that prepared by Apicius, a renowned gastronome who lived during Roman times, or think of a pork chop or roast prepared in the same way. Other meats can also be roasted with a honey caramel. Keep in mind, however, that the technique is delicate—the caramel should not burn.

Of course, honey can be used for cakes. For this, choose your honey primarily for its consistency and keep in mind that if it is not liquid, it should be melted very gently before using. The honeys of Provence have exceptional flavors, particularly acacia and linden flower honeys which add flavor without being too strong and heady. For pastries, other possibilities include lavender honey, very sweet and aromatic, "multi-flower" honey, or rosemary honey, even if the latter can occasionally be a little strong. For savory cooking, avoid dark honeys, such as pine honey. However, heather honey can be very pleasant. In general, opt more for lighter honeys.

In any case, whether for savory dishes or pastries, honey adds aroma, sweetness, and exquisite flavor.

THE TIAN:
PROVENÇAL CASSEROLE COOKERY

A tian always includes a mixture of vegetables, often from the family garden.

« The Provençal word *tian*, like the american word *casserole* or the general word *dish*, means both the container and its contents. Jacques Chibois explains that "traditionally, this was cooking for poor families who could mix in whatever they had available and bake it to make a whole meal. Some included only vegetables, but a bit of leftover meat or fish could be added, salt cod for example. These gratins often rounded up the last vegetables from the autumn garden. This was the original oven-to-table approach which mingled all the flavors so beautifully thanks to the long, slow cooking." As if often the case in Provençal cuisine, the *tian* could be reheated and was even better the second time around. Some cooks served a baked dish like this hot one day and at room temperature with a simple salad the next. A housewife thus prepared two or three meals in one, giving each its own style and flavor. The *tian* is Provence's version of old-fashioned, grassroots slow food.

Provençal historian and poet Frédéric Mistral records in his almanac of Provençal folklore how *tians* were used in the nineteenth century. He defines the *tian* simply as a "dish cooked in the oven, a gratin" or elsewhere as "a large, shallow earthenware dish which in some parts of the country is named in Provençal *gavette* or *graal*." In another article, he explains, "The veritable *tian* comes from the town of Carpentras and it is a mishmash of greens like chard, spinach, parsley, and purslane cooked with cod or some other fish, garlic, salt and pepper, baked with eggs, cheese, perhaps milk and above all olive oil. Some cooks used hard-boiled eggs, cut into slices to make a mosaic or arabesque on top, with a sprinkling of breadcrumbs. When that came out of the oven, all golden, you would give anything for just a bite!"

Before ovens were common in private homes, *tians* were usually cooked by the village baker. When his bread finished baking and the oven was still hot, he could put everyone's dishes in and cook them for hours if necessary. Mistral tells the sad tale of a Camargue fisherman who had no *tian* nor any other food at Carnival time, when everyone else was feasting. Reduced to eating whatever he could find on the beach and the snails from his thatched roof, he watched the housewives of the village pass by, "all on their way to Maître Crubèsi, the baker who had the best reputation for cooking *tians*, which they were carrying his way in the early morning hours. Each was anxious to reserve a place in his oven also for their *fougasses*, their cakes, their potato gratins, their almond clusters, their stuffed geese, and their terrines, those huge pâtés in pastry cases. A bit before noon, the ladies passed by again, this time with their dishes, their *tians* and their *tourtes* just fresh from the oven, everything steaming and fragrant, nicely risen and cooked just right. The whole village was filled with the aroma of food." Let's hope that someone remembered to invite the poor fisherman!

For many people in Provence, the *tian* brings back memories of childhood. René Jouveau, in his book on grassroots Provençal cooking, recalls his grandmother in the village of Védène making a delicious pumpkin *tian*. "I admired the even cut of those shiny little

Earthenware tian
dishes are waiting to
be filled at the Pavillon
de Galon.

golden cubes which fell from her knife, like
buildings stones for some miniature edifice. This
multitude was rolled in flour in a clean tea cloth,
then placed in a well-oiled gratin dish, seasoned
with garlic and chopped parsley, salt, and pepper.
It went into the oven just like that, without any
liquid, and came out only when the top was
almost charred. This is not a dish that will fatten
you up but it is part of the spiritual nourishment
beloved by the poets of the South," he says.

The kind of cooking required by a *tian* is hard to
incorporate into the logic of a gastronomic
restaurant but perfectly adapted to family fare.
Jacques Chibois often ate *tians* as a child both
at home in Limoges and in his mother's
neighborhood bistro. He considers that this style is
appropriate for cold climates or winter dishes. In
Provence today, he says, "fashion favors a quicker,
fresher, more expressive cooking—just a bit of oil
on a tomato with herbs and spices is enough." But
he is happy to have experience in both modes:
slow food family style and the new Provençal
approach of quick, fresh preparation. He can
appreciate both the strong flavors of
grandmotherly cuisine and today's evolution
towards a lighter delicacy.

Tian of Provençal vegetables

For 6 servings: 4 tablespoons (2 ounces) raw rice, 2¼ pounds zucchini, 1 bunch swiss chard, 2 onions, 1 clove garlic, 3 tablespoons olive oil, 3 eggs, salt, pepper, 2 ounces lean bacon or ham, chopped fresh basil or parsley, ½ cup (2 ounces) grated parmesan cheese, 1 bunch squash blossoms

The tian

Cook the rice for 10 minutes in a saucepan of salted boiling water (1½ tablespoons salt for 1 quart water). Rinse under warm water and drain thoroughly.

Peel the zucchini, cut into large pieces, and cook in a pan of salted boiling water for 5 to 8 minutes, depending upon the age of the vegetables. Drain and pass through a food mill or process coarsely. Remove the ribs from the chard and coarsely chop the leaves.

Preheat the oven to 345°F. Peel and chop the onions. Peel and crush the garlic. Sauté onion and garlic in a skillet with 2 tablespoons of the olive oil. Add the chard and zucchini to the skillet.

Beat the eggs with salt and pepper. Chop the bacon finely and add to the eggs with the basil or parsley and the Parmesan cheese. Combine the egg mixture with the vegetables and add the rice. Chop the squash blossoms and add to the mixture. Taste for seasoning. Turn the mixture into an oiled gratin dish. Cook in the preheated oven for 45 minutes. At the end of the cooking, increase the oven temperature for about 10 minutes to lightly brown the top.

CHEF'S NOTE

A one-dish meal, the tian *can be served hot or cold. In winter, zucchini can be replaced by other winter squash.*

Roast kid

with sorrel sauce and stuffed baby vegetables

FOR 4 SERVINGS:
— FOR THE GOAT: ½ KID* OF 2½ TO 3 POUNDS (ASK YOUR BUTCHER TO PREPARE THE GOAT, SEPARATING THE LEG AND THE RACK, RESERVING THE BONES AND TRIMMINGS FOR THE SAUCE), SALT, PEPPER, 5 CLOVES GARLIC, 3½ TABLESPOONS SOFTENED UNSALTED BUTTER, 2 TABLESPOONS OLIVE OIL, A FEW BAY LEAVES, A FEW SAVORY LEAVES, A FEW SPRIGS THYME
— FOR THE SAUCE: 1 WHITE ONION, 3 CLOVES GARLIC, 1 SPRIG THYME, 1 SPRIG ROSEMARY, A FEW SAVORY LEAVES, 1 BAY LEAF, 2 TABLESPOONS DRY WHITE WINE, ⅔ CUP CREAM, SALT, PEPPER, 5 LEAVES SORREL, A FEW DROPS LEMON JUICE.
— FOR THE VEGETABLES: ½ POUND NEW *GRENAILLE*** POTATOES (OR OTHER WAXY BOILING POTATOES), 8 SMALL NEW ONIONS, 8 WHITE TURNIPS WITH THEIR LEAVES, 2 TABLESPOONS OLIVE OIL, 1 BAY LEAF, 1 SPRIG ROSEMARY, 1½ TABLESPOONS UNSALTED BUTTER, SALT, PEPPER, 7 OUNCES SHELLED FAVA BEANS
— FOR THE STUFFED BABY VEGETABLES: 6 ROUND ZUCCHINI, 6 PATTYPAN SQUASH, 6 SMALL TOMATOES, 4 TABLESPOONS OLIVE OIL, 2 GARLIC CLOVES, 5 SLICES SANDWICH BREAD, 3 TABLESPOONS MILK, 1 CUP FRESHLY GRATED PARMESAN CHEESE, 3 BEATEN EGGS, 10 TABLESPOONS CHOPPED PARSLEY, 3 TABLESPOONS CHOPPED FRESH BASIL, SALT, PEPPER, 6 ZUCCHINI BLOSSOMS, 1 CUBE POULTRY BOUILLON

The kid

Preheat the oven to 410°F. Season the kid with salt and pepper. Peel the garlic, cut 4 cloves into pointed spikes, cut 1 clove in half. Stud the kid leg with the garlic spikes, then rub the leg and rack with the softened butter. Place the leg and rack, with bones and trimmings, in a roasting pan and brush with 1 tablespoon olive oil and brown on the stove. Place in the oven and roast 12 to 15 minutes for the rack, 30 minutes for the leg. Transfer the meats to a rack, cover with aluminum foil, and let rest in a warm oven (turned off). Prepare the sauce.

Just before serving, preheat the oven to 400°F. Return the meat to the roasting pan with the bay leaves, savory, thyme, and the remaining garlic clove. Spoon the remaining tablespoon of oil over all and return the pan to the hot oven for 5 minutes.

The sauce

Peel and chop the onion. Crush the garlic cloves in their skins. Place the roasting pan on the stove with the bones and trimmings. Add the onion,

garlic, thyme, rosemary, savory, and bay leaf, and brown, stirring. Deglaze with the white wine, add 1¼ cups water and boil for 10 to 12 minutes. Strain the juice and transfer to a small saucepan. Reduce over low heat, then add the cream. Season with salt and pepper, bring to a boil, and remove form the heat. Just before serving, rinse and chop the sorrel leaves, and add to the sauce with the lemon juice.

The vegetables

Peel the potatoes, onions, and turnips (leaving on turnip stems and leaves). Sauté the potatoes in a skillet with 1 tablespoon of the olive oil, bay leaf, and rosemary. Cook the turnips in a large saucepan of boiling salted water (1½ tablespoon salt for 1 quart water) for 8 to 10 minutes, depending upon their size. Plunge them into cold water and drain immediately. Place the onions in a small saucepan with 1 tablespoon water, the butter, salt, and pepper. Cover and cook for 10 minutes.

Drop the fava beans into a saucepan of boiling salted water (1½ tablespoons salt for 1 quart water). When the water returns to a boil, remove the beans, plunge them into cold water, and drain immediately. Remove the outer skin of the fava beans and place them in a saucepan with the turnips and onions. Before serving, reheat with 1 tablespoon olive oil and 1 tablespoon water.

The stuffed baby vegetables

Slice off the tops of the zucchini, pattypan, and tomatoes (about ¼ of their height), reserving the tops. Hollow out the vegetables, dicing the flesh of the zucchini and pattypan into small cubes, and reserving tomato flesh for another use. Plunge the hollowed out zucchini and pattypans, with their tops, into a saucepan of boiling salted water for 4 minutes. Drain well. Sauté the cubed zucchini and pattypan in 2 tablespoons olive oil, and let cool.

Peel, crush, and mince the garlic. Dice the sandwich bread, crusts removed. Soak the bread in the milk. Add the sautéed squash, Parmesan cheese, eggs, parsley, basil, garlic, salt, and pepper and mix together. Stuff the vegetables with this mixture. Replace the tops and place on a baking sheet.

Preheat the oven to 400°F. Boil a little water with the bouillon cube and the remaining olive oil, and drizzle over the vegetables. Cover with aluminum foil and cook for 20 minutes.

Presentation

Slice the leg and rack and arrange them attractively on a serving dish. Arrange the vegetables in a ring around the meat. Spoon a ribbon of the sauce over all and serve the remaining sauce on the side.

* Kid or young goat, *is as delicate and tender as young lamb. Spring lamb (preferably milk-fed) can be substituted.*

** Grenaille *potatoes are small waxy boiling potatoes with a buttery-yellow flesh and a nutty flavor. Substitute the most flavorful new boiling potatoes available.*

CHEF'S NOTE

Prepare the baby vegetables and their stuffing, and cook them in advance—this way they can be easily reheated in a baking dish with a drizzle of olive oil.

The Chef's Advice
SAUTÉING POTATOES

The first thing to know is that the best oils for sautéing potatoes are those with the least taste. If you decide to use an olive oil, choose an oil from the second pressing. But even more appropriate for this method of cooking are peanut oil or grape seed oil. In general, if the fat or oil used for frying does not hold up well to high temperatures, the potatoes cooked in it will be heavy and indigestible.

Heat the skillet and add the oil. Then add the potatoes, well dried, and salt them immediately so that the salt penetrates deeply into the potato.

Turn the potatoes several times in the skillet so that all sides cauterize or sear, then continue cooking over low heat. Partially cover (covering completely will prevent the potatoes from browning and will make them become mushy); in this way they will continue to brown, while releasing a little steam. Turn them from time to time, but not too much (or the potatoes won't brown and will crumble).

When they are about three-fourths cooked, add the butter or duck fat and aromatics (rosemary and other dried herbs) or garlic in its skin, etc., to give the desired flavor. If these flavor elements had been added at the beginning of the cooking, they would have burned and all of their flavors would have been lost. Follow these little tips and you will be ready to prepare the best imaginable sautéed potatoes.

WEDDINGS, THEN AND NOW

AY IN PROVENCE WAS TRADITIONALLY consecrated to the virgin Mary, a month for courtship but not weddings, which began in June. A beau might declare himself through symbolic gifts—bouquets of special flowers or saffron breads, which a girl might accept or refuse as she wished. Until the French Revolution of 1789, actual abduction was not unknown. A new law making a witnessed marriage contract obligatory at least guaranteed the bride's consent! In the following century, the groom buried his bachelorhood in a mock funeral ceremony while his beloved received women friends and relations to show off her elegant trousseau. Both events involved good eating, as did the "contract signing" the night before the ceremony. On the day itself, in June or thereafter, traditional weddings were celebrated at church in the morning, then followed by a banquet that lasted until the gala ball in the evening.

The wedding itself involved many colorful customs. The bride's dress must not enter her house before the morning of the ceremony itself. To drive off bad luck, the family put salt in the bride's pockets and in the groom's shoes. If, before the altar, the young man was able to kneel on the edge of his fiancée's dress as it spread around her, this meant he would dominate in the marriage. But if she wished to maintain her authority, she bent her finger as the ring was slipped onto it. On leaving the church, the newlyweds passed under a flowery arch, accompanied by Provençal musicians. If the family had roots in the Camargue region, two rows of cowboys made the arch with their "tridents," the goads used for herding. Children waiting at the bottom of the church steps cried out, "*Vivo li nòvi!*" ("Long live the newlyweds!") They expected to be showered with sugared almonds and coins, but if the harvest was too scant, the children added, "*Es malant, lou nòvi, es malant! A manja de coucourdo e lou bouioun i a fa mau!*" ("The groom is ailing, the groom is ailing! He ate too much pumpkin and it has made him wobbly!") Presumably, no young man would court such humiliation.

Musicians playing tambourines and fifes participate in all traditional festivities.

Elisabeth Barbier, in her serial novel *Les Gens de Mogador*, traces the life of an old Provençal family. She recounts a wedding supper starting off "with that rather stiff pace suitable for such an occasion, which loosened up when they got to the roast." Was this the moment when the best man was expected to take off the bride's garter? After the meal, "the matriarch of the family received her outmoded and fawning female relations" while the young people opened the ball.

Today, Provençal weddings usually take place in the afternoon. Do people have less stamina than their ancestors? Some guests are invited only for drinks, others stay on for dinner, but an experienced caterer says he always provides one or two tables for those who linger obstinately. Sometimes etiquette is complicated, as with the father of one bride who wanted his champagne served only to the guests of his own family, not the groom's! The old-fashioned bridal crown that was once preserved under glass has now been replaced with a crown of fresh orange blossoms. The bride's elegant dress is now, as then, in the latest style. According to expert Michel Biehn, antique wedding dresses provide some of our best clues to

fashions gone by. Until the Second Empire (1860), brides wore green rather than white. Green was the color of hope, and also symbolized the young girl's independence. Hélène Costa, who created the Provençal Museum of Costumes and Jewelry in Grasse, says that the green wedding dress on display there belonged to the mother of her great-great grandmother who married at eighteen in 1843.

Many wedding suppers are held at the Bastide Saint-Antoine. Jacques Chibois feels that Southerners know how to celebrate and enjoy formal occasions. Weddings are still much appreciated in Provence, even if the couple has been living together for some time and counts among the guests their own children! Today the delights still start the evening before with a "very simple and relaxed" family dinner. Chibois explains that on the day itself, the families often have a big brunch on the terrace "because they know they will not eat again before evening. At noon, they will have to dress and go to the church for the wedding mass. Around 6:30, there will be a cocktail party with lots of different canapés, if possible in the garden. Then the oldsters can gossip in quiet corners while the children run around at will. The banquet itself is held around 8:30 in the evening and may well last until midnight. After that, the fun begins."

Above:
One of many dresses displayed at the Provençal Costume and Jewelry Museum in Grasse.

Right:
Folk costumes varied according to the town, age and social origin of the wearer.

Bruno Gedda is a musical stylist and disc jockey who specializes in weddings in Provence. Elegant socialites and international celebrities seek him out for these special occasions. He remarks that many customs have disappeared, but the bride and her father still open the ball. The newlyweds slip off a bit later, pursued or not by indiscreet jokers. Bruno's job is to "keep lighting the fire" through the night until dawn. But by then, if two or three couples want to stay forever, he plays progressively slower music, at a lower volume.

"And the next day," says Chibois, "the whole family comes for a *soupe au pistou* (basil vegetable soup) or *tians* with salads, simple food for the morning after."

Sea scallops
with almond milk

For 4 servings:

— For the chickpea purée: 1¼ cups chickpea flour, salt, pepper, 6 tablespoons olive oil, 1½ tablespoons unsalted butter, 1 teaspoon freshly grated parmesan cheese

— For the vegetable sauce: ½ fennel bulb, 2 new onions, 2 tablespoons olive oil, 2 cloves garlic, 1 pinch fennel seeds, 1 pinch grated nutmeg, zest of 1 untreated lemon, zest of 1 untreated orange, 1 pinch powdered turmeric, 1 tablespoon orange juice, 1½ tablespoons softened unsalted butter, a few drops lemon juice

— For the scallops: 20 plump, very fresh sea scallops, 1 pinch curry powder, salt, pepper, 1 clove garlic, 1 tablespoon olive oil

— For the almond milk: ½ cup cream, a few drops amaretto (almond liqueur)

— For the presentation: paprika flakes

Chickpea purée

Place the chickpea flour in mixing bowl with a little salt and pepper. Gradually add 2 cups water and the olive oil, stirring constantly with a wooden spoon to obtain a smooth, fluid batter with the consistency of a crepe batter. Pour the mixture into a saucepan and warm over medium heat, stirring and whisking constantly. When the mixture thickens, incorporate the butter and Parmesan cheese.

The vegetable jus

Rinse and chop the fennel. Peel and chop the onions. Sauté the fennel and onions in a skillet with 1 tablespoon olive oil. Peel and crush the garlic cloves and add to the skillet along with the fennel seeds, nutmeg, lemon and orange zests, and the turmeric. Add 1 cup water and the orange juice and cook for 15 minutes over low heat. Strain the vegetable juices into a saucepan and cook over low heat until reduced to about ½ cup. Whisk in the butter, 1 tablespoon olive oil and, at the last minute, the lemon juice.

The scallops

Pat the scallops dry. Mix the curry, salt, and pepper together and sprinkle over the scallops. Crush the garlic clove in its skin. Heat the olive oil in a skillet, add the garlic and sauté the scallops quickly on both sides until nicely browned.

Almond milk

Heat the cream in a saucepan with the Amaretto. Just before serving, process or blend the almond milk until foamy.

Presentation

Spoon 5 teaspoons of the chickpea purée in a ring around the center of each serving plate and top each dot of purée with a scallop. Spoon the vegetable juices and a ribbon of the foamy almond milk around each serving. Decorate with paprika flakes.

CHEF'S NOTE

For a nice mousse with a little body, emulsify the almond milk in a processor or blender at the last minute.

Apricots in almond purses

For 4 servings:
— For the apricot sauce: 8 apricot halves in syrup, 1 drop vanilla extract
— For the glazed almonds: 1 egg white, ¾ cup powdered sugar, a few drops lemon juice, ⅓ cup whole almonds
— For the beggar's purses: 14 tablespoons unsalted butter divided, ⅔ cup granulated sugar, 1 cup ground almonds, 2 eggs (at room temperature), 2½ tablespoons flour, 1 tablespoon apricot brandy, 4 apricot halves in syrup, 1 drop vanilla extract, 1 tablespoon honey, 4 sheets phyllo pastry
— For the presentation: powdered sugar, apricot wedges (optional)

Apricot sauce

Process the apricots to a purée with 3 tablespoons of their syrup and the liquid vanilla. Refrigerate covered.

Glazed almonds

Preheat the oven to 320°F. Combine the egg white, powdered sugar and lemon juice, and mix together until smooth. Brush the almonds with this mixture. Place them on a baking sheet covered with baking parchment and cook for 35 minutes, until golden brown. Set aside in a dry place or store in an airtight box.

Beggar's purses

Prepare the almond cream: In a mixing bowl, cream together 8 tablespoons softened butter and the sugar. Add the ground almonds and eggs. Add the flour and whisk until smooth. Add the apricot brandy.

Cut the apricots into cubes, and sauté in a skillet with 1½ tablespoons butter until golden brown. Add the vanilla and let cool. Delicately mix the apricots with the almond cream. Divide the mixture in 8 equal parts and form 8 balls. Refrigerate for 1 hour until firm.

Preheat the oven to 350°F. Warm the honey with 4 tablespoons butter, melted, and brush half of the mixture over 1 sheet of phyllo. Cover with a second sheet of phyllo. Repeat this procedure with the remaining two sheets of phyllo. Cut each double sheet into eight 6-inch squares (2 squares per serving). Place one chilled ball of apricot-almond cream in the center of each square and draw up the corners, gently squeezing together in the center to form a beggar's purse. Place on a well-buttered baking sheet and cook in the preheated oven for 10 minutes.

Presentation

Delicately remove the beggar's purses from the baking sheet using a spatula and sprinkle each with powdered sugar. Place on serving plates. Spoon a ribbon of the apricot sauce around the purses and top with the glazed almonds. Garnish with apricot wedges if desired.

CHEF'S NOTE

Keep the phyllo in its package, taking out the leaves one at a time, as needed, since they dry out quickly in contact with the air and become impossible to work with. Cook the beggar's purses on a silicon baking sheet; they will be easier to remove.

FOOD SHOPPING IN NICE IN 1764

*Above right:
Riviera markets,
then and now.*

Tobias George Smollett, one of Britain's best eighteenth-century novelists, settled in Nice in 1764 for his health. He proved to be an excellent observer of the food chain from the moment of arrival (Letter XIII, January 15, 1764). "When I stand upon the rampart and look round me, I can scarce help thinking myself enchanted. The small extent of country which I see, is all cultivated like a garden. Indeed, the plain presents nothing but gardens, full of green trees loaded with oranges, lemons, citrons, and bergamots, which make a delightful appearance. If you examine them more nearly, you will find plantations of green pease ready to gather; all sorts of sallading and pot-herbs in perfection; and plats of roses, carnations, ranunculus, anemone, and daffodils, blowing in full glory with such beauty, vigour, and perfume, as no flower in England ever exhibited." Smollett chose a lodging in town which would allow him to enjoy country flavors every day (Letter XVIII, September 2, 1764). "I have likewise two small gardens, well stocked with oranges, lemons, peaches, figs, grapes, corinths, sallad, and potherbs." He wanted to learn everything about local economy, especially the making of olive oil and wine. He relished the Nice markets and listed their wares with evident delight. In September, for example, he found the stands "tolerably well supplied. Their beef—which comes from Piedmont— is pretty good, and we have it all the year. In the winter, we have likewise excellent pork and delicate lamb; but the mutton is indifferent. Piedmont also affords us delicious capons, fed with maize; and this country produces excellent turkeys, but very few geese. . . . Autumn and winter are the seasons for game; hares, partridges, quails, wild-pigeons, woodcocks, snipes, thrushes, beccaficas, and ortolans. Wild-boar is sometimes found in the mountains: It has a delicious taste, not unlike that of the wild hog in Jamaica." Further on, he found the seafood, "Nice is not without variety of fish; though they are not counted so good in their kinds as those of the ocean. Soals, and flatfish in general, are scarce. Here are some mullets, both grey and red. We

245 — GRASSE
Maraîchères de la Place aux Herbes

sometimes see the dory, which is called St. Pierre; with rockfish, bonita, and mackarel. The gurnard appears pretty often; and there is plenty of a kind of large whiting, which eats pretty well, but has not the delicacy of that which is caught on our coast. One of the best fish of this country, is called *le loup*, about two or three pounds in weight; white, firm, and well-flavoured. . . . Here too are found the *vyvre*, or, as we call it, weaver; remarkable for its long, sharp spines, so dangerous to the fingers of the fishermen. We have abundance of the *sœpie*, or cuttlefish, of which the people in this country make a delicate ragout; as also of the *polype de mer*, which is an ugly animal, with long feelers, like tails, which they often wind about the legs of the fishermen. They are stewed with onions, and eat something like cow-heel. The market sometimes affords the *ecrevisse de mer*, which is a lobster without claws, of a sweetish taste; and there are a few rock oysters, very small and very rank" (Letter XVIII, September 2 1764).

It is amusing but also daunting to compare this choice with today's selections. Smollett paid equal attention to fruit and vegetables, an

uncommon attitude in his century. Again, he stressed the relationships sometimes forgotten in modern times among a product, its origins, and its best season. For example, in Letter XIX, October 10, 1764, he wrote, "In the winter, we have green pease, asparagus, artichokes, cauliflower, beans, French beans, celery, and endive; cabbage, coleworts, radishes, turnips, carrots, betteraves, sorrel, lettuce, onions, garlic, and chalot. We have potatoes from the mountains, mushrooms, champignons, and truffles. Piedmont affords white truffles, counted the most delicious in the world: they sell for about three livres the pound. The fruits of this season are pickled olives, oranges, lemons, citrons, citronelles, dried figs, grapes, apples, pears, almonds, chestnuts, walnuts, filberts, medlars, pomegranates, and a fruit called azeroiles, about the size of a nutmeg, of an oblong shape, red colour, and agreeable acid taste. I might likewise add the cherry of the *laurus cerasus*, which is sold in the market; very beautiful to the eye, but insipid to the palate. In summer we have all those vegetables in perfection. There is also a kind of small courge, or gourd, of which the people of the country made a very savoury ragout, with the help of eggs, cheese, and fresh anchovies. Another is made of the *badenjean*, which the Spaniards call *berengena* (eggplant). It is much eaten in Spain and the Levant, as well as by the Moors in Barbary. It is about the size and shape of a hen's egg, inclosed in a cup like an acorn; when ripe, of a faint purple colour. It grows on a stalk about a foot high, with long spines. . . . There are some caper bushes in this neighbourhood, which grow wild in holes of garden walls, and require no sort of cultivation; in one or two gardens, there are palm-trees; but the dates never ripen."

Smollet also observed some unusual ways in which the locals consumed their produce. "Among the refreshments of these warm countries, I ought not to forget mentioning the sorbettes, which are sold in coffee-houses, and places of public resort. They are iced froth, made with juice of oranges, apricots, or peaches; very agreeable to the palate, and so extremely cold, that I was afraid to swallow them in this hot country, until I found from information and experience, that they may be taken in moderation, without any bad consequence" (Letter XIX, October 10 1764).

A doctor himself, Smollett sometimes worried about his health to the point of hypochondria. But he also sought pleasure, and not only in his food. Another enjoyment, rare for his time, was swimming in the

Above:
Cabbage and other
heirloom vegetables
in the potager at
Val Joanis.

sea. He admired the "fine open beach, extending several miles to the westward of Nice" (Letter XXIII, November 19, 1764). He advised bathing, however, "with great precaution, as the sea is very deep, and the descent very abrupt from within a yard or two of the water's edge. The people here were much surprised when I began to bathe in the beginning of May. They thought it very strange, that a man seemingly consumptive, should plunge into the sea, especially when the weather was so cold; and some of the doctors prognosticated immediate death." But, when it was perceived that he seemed better as a result, others followed suit. Smollett regrets that "the fair sex must be intirely excluded" from this activity, "unless they lay aside all regard to decorum; for the shore is always lined with fishing-boats and crouded with people." This writer's chronicle allows us to enjoy piquant contrasts between his times and ours, and his observations provide precious insights into the food history of Provence.

Excerpts from Tobias Smollett: *Travels Through France and Italy*, Oxford World Classics, editor Frank Felenstein, 1979.

Pearls of garden peas
with morel mushrooms and baby beet leaves

FOR 4 SERVINGS:

— FOR THE MORELS: 1 POUND FRESH MOREL MUSHROOMS, 1 LARGE SHALLOT, 1½ TABLESPOONS UNSALTED BUTTER, 2 TABLESPOONS NOILLY PRAT (OR OTHER DRY WHITE VERMOUTH), 2 TABLESPOONS RED PORT, ⅓ OUNCE (¼ CUP) DRIED MOREL MUSHROOMS, ¾ CUP CREAM, 1 TEASPOON CHOPPED FRESH TARRAGON, 1 TABLESPOON DRY WHITE WINE, A FEW DROPS LEMON JUICE

— FOR THE PEAS: 2 OUNCES SNOW PEAS, 5½ OUNCES (1⅓ CUP) SHELLED FRESH GARDEN PEAS, 1 PINCH POWDERED POULTRY STOCK, SALT

— FOR THE PRESENTATION: BABY SPINACH LEAVES (OR OTHER DISTINCTIVE SALAD GREENS SUCH AS LAMB'S LETTUCE OR DANDELION GREENS)

The morels

Rinse the morels and trim the stem ends. Peel and chop the shallot, and sweat in the butter in a small skillet. Deglaze with the vermouth and the Port. Chop the dried morels finely and combine with the cream, then add to the skillet along with the fresh morels. Cover and cook for 12 to 15 minutes over low heat. At the end of the cooking, add the chopped tarragon. Just before serving, whisk the sauce, adding the white wine and lemon juice for a fresh finish.

The peas

Cook the snow peas for 3 minutes in a saucepan of boiling salted water (1½ tablespoons salt for 1 quart water), then plunge them into cold water. Drain thoroughly. Cook the garden peas in the same manner and drain. To serve, reheat the snow peas and the garden peas in a saucepan with a little water, the powdered poultry stock and a pinch of salt. Bring to a boil for a few minutes.

Presentation

Rinse and dry the beet greens. Arrange the garden peas neatly around the edge of each serving plate. Add the morels, spoon the sauce around, and garnish with the snow peas and beet greens.

CHEF'S NOTE

If fresh morel mushrooms are not available, use dried morels soaked in cold water. Trim the stems, cut in half, and cook in the same way as the fresh morels.

Quail breast
with Provençal spelt and Nice-style vegetables

For 4 servings:
— For the quails: 6 plump quails (3 breasts per person, depending upon the size), salt, pepper, 1 tablespoon olive oil, 1 tablespoon tapenade*
— For the jus: 2 shallots, 1 carrot, 1 slice (¾ ounce) celery root, 2 garlic cloves, 2 tablespoons olive oil, 2 sprigs dried fennel, 1 sprig thyme, 1 bay leaf, ¼ cup marc de provence**, a few slices dried cèpe mushrooms, 4 star anise, 1½ tablespoons unsalted butter, salt, pepper
— For the vegetables: 1 fennel bulb, 4 purple artichokes, ½ lemon, 2 small zucchini with their flowers, 2 garlic cloves, ½ cup precooked spelt, salt, 1 pinch powdered poultry bouillon, 1 pinch ground cumin, 1 tablespoon tomato paste, 5 leaves fresh sage, 2½ tablespoons olive oil, 2½ tablespoons grated parmesan cheese, 1 tablespoon unsalted butter, 1 large eggplant (or 4 mini-eggplants), pepper.
— Presentation: a few sage leaves

The quails

Have your butcher prepare the quails, removing the breasts with the wings, and breaking up the carcasses and legs for the sauce. Refrigerate the breasts until all of the other elements of the recipe are ready. Shortly before serving, salt and pepper the quail breasts. In a nonstick skillet, heat the olive oil and brown the quail breasts and wings, skin-side down. Turn and brown the other side for 30 seconds; the meat should remain rare. Remove the quail, cover with aluminum foil and let rest on a rack in a warm oven (turned off). Brush each breast with the tapenade. Just before serving, reheat in the oven for 4 to 5 minutes at 350°F.

The jus

Peel and coarsely chop the shallots, carrot, and celery root. Peel and crush the garlic cloves. Heat 1 tablespoon olive oil in a skillet and sauté the quail legs and carcasses with the shallots, carrot, and the celery root. Add the dried fennel sprigs, the garlic cloves, thyme, and bay leaf. When well browned, flame with the marc de Provence. Add ¾ cup water and

the dried cèpes, and cook for 25 minutes over low heat. Strain the juice into a saucepan and reduce over low heat to about ½ cup. Add the star anise and let infuse for 1 to 2 minutes; remove. Incorporate the butter and remaining 1 tablespoon olive oil, whisking constantly. Season with salt and pepper and keep warm in a double boiler.

The vegetables

Rinse the fennel bulb and cut in quarters. Remove the outer leaves of the artichokes, keeping the bottom, heart, and about 2 inches of the stem. Rub with lemon juice and cut each artichoke in half lengthwise. Rinse the zucchini and cut into large cubes, reserving the flowers. Peel and chop the garlic. Combine the vegetables with the spelt in a saucepan and add 1¼ cups boiling water. Season with salt, add the powdered poultry bouillon, cumin, tomato paste and garlic. Cook for 20 minutes over low heat.

Remove the zucchini, fennel, and artichokes successively when each is cooked and set them aside, leaving the spelt in the pan. Chop the sage leaves and add to the pan with 1 tablespoon olive oil, the Parmesan, and butter, stirring with a wooden spoon to obtain a creamy mixture.

Preheat the oven to 355°F. Rinse the eggplant and cut lengthwise into four quarters. (If using mini eggplants, cut each in half.) Season with salt and pepper, then place the eggplant pieces flesh-side down on a baking sheet brushed with 1 tablespoon olive oil. Bake for 15 (for the mini-eggplants) or 20 (for the large) minutes. Sauté the squash blossoms in the remaining olive oil.

Presentation

Arrange the quail breasts on the serving plates. Surround with the vegetables and spelt, spoon the sauce over and decorate with sage leaves and squash blossoms.

* Tapenade *is a thick, flavorful Provençal purée of ripe black olives, capers, anchovies, and lemon juice.*

** Marc de Provence *is white or clear brandy from Provence. Subtitute any good quality brandy, preferably clear.*

CHEF'S NOTE

Spelt, an ancient cereal grain, is wrongly considered to be the ancestor of wheat. More rustic than the latter, spelt once grew in many parts of Provence, including the northeast of the Vaucluse and the southwest of the Alpes de Haute Provence regions, as well as in certain areas of the Drome and the Hautes-Alpes areas. Rich in nutrients, it was widely used in the past for making bread. When cooked with other vegetables, it makes a delicious side dish.

The Chef's Advice

COOKING VEGETABLES IN WATER

The best way to cook vegetables, if you want to respect their nature, is in a large quantity of salted water.

Add 1½ tablespoons salt for 1 quart of water; this will seal the vegetables and prevent their mineral salts from dissolving as the temperature rapidly increases.

Next, let the vegetables cook uncovered to allow the carbonic gases to escape. If covered, the vegetables will change color. It is for this reason that cooking vegetables in a pressure cooker, even beans and other dried legumes, is a true crime.

When the vegetables are cooked to your taste, remove them immediately, drain in a colander, then plunge them immediately into ice water, or water with ice cubes, for just a second. The cold stops the cooking. Because of this thermal shock—just a second is enough—green vegetables become even greener, carrots turn a brighter orange, and so forth. Don't let the vegetables soak in the cold water, this will drain them of their mineral salts.

It is best to avoid cooking vegetables by steam. There are many foods that can be successfully cooked by this method, but not vegetables. Steam, of course, is water set into motion and it washes vegetables, removing all of their chlorophyll. On the other hand, if they are protected, enveloped, for example, they will retain all of their nutritional properties.

Cooked in this way, or blanched simply in water, vegetables are excellent and ready to be finished and garnished according to each cook's taste.

A Garden in Provence

«... the garden, that paradise of the marvellous variety of things, of rich sensations procured, of choices offered in the quality, philosophy and art of living ...»

Francis Ponge

THE ROSE OF GRASSE

The May rose (Rose de mai) is a variety adapted to southern climates.

FOR CENTURIES, VISITORS TO GRASSE admired the surrounding terraces where flowers were grown for the perfume industry. In 1778, Abbé Papon described the "delicious fragrance" of orange trees, lemon, and citron intermingled with Spanish jasmine. In 1838, the novelist Stendhal was entranced by the "cultivated fields of roses." Some perfumers in Grasse still use locally grown blossoms to create scents famous round the world. The legendary Joy of Patou, for example, is essentially a blending of rose and jasmine fragrances.

The gardens of the region have sometimes been enhanced by these plantings. In *Perfume from Provence* (1935), Lady Fortescue describes her beds of roses edged with lavender, set off against a commercial plantation of orange trees underplanted with jasmine. Moreover, an English rose-grower had forewarned her that ramblers on the Riviera would far surpass in scent and vigor those she had known at home. "Madam, you have never seen a climbing rose until you have seen it in the South of France," he told her, "Here in England we haven't sun enough!"

The rose grown for the perfume industry is the May rose or *Rose de mai*, a hybrid of *Rosa gallica* and *Rosa centifolia*. Today's crop comes from a nearly thornless variety introduced in 1895 by the Nabonnand nursery. This family enterprise also created two of the most beautiful old-fashioned cultivars still found locally in country gardens: the shrubby Général Schablikine and the rambling Sénateur Lafollette often seen meandering through the massive crowns of olive trees. The Nabonnands' May rose is generally single-flowered, though there is also a double sport with up to a hundred petals. It is cultivated on its own rootstock or grafted onto *Rosa indica Major* or *Rosa frédica*. The latter was developed by the French Agronomy Institute (INRA) in the town of Fréjus, which crossed *Indica Major* with *Multiflora* to obtain earlier flowering. These rootstocks are both adapted to the

8   *SUR LA CÔTE D'AZUR. — La Cueillette des Roses. — LL.*

Mediterranean climate, unlike *Rosa canina*, the one most common in Northern Europe. Many southern gardeners who import their roses from England meet with disappointment because their acquisitions have been grafted onto an unsuitable rootstock.

For centuries, the rose industry was a family affair involving small holdings. Picking petals at dawn was women's work. A single plantation could be expected to last a dozen years, reaching full production after four or five. A good picker might harvest five to eight kilos of petals (twelve to twenty pounds) per hour. Nine hundred kilos of petals are needed to produce one kilo of essence. At the beginning of the eighteenth century, scents were obtained by distillation carried out right in the fields thanks to portable stills mounted on wagons. The essence was extracted from the petals using water vapor, but the flowers, heated directly over the fire, were often burned. Even when this did not happen, certain elements of the fragrance resist vapor treatment, others change when exposed to heat, and still others dissolved and could not be recuperated. A more subtle technique was required.

The invention of *enfleurage* allowed the reconstitution of the most fragile fragrances and brought wealth and fame to the city of Grasse. Petals were now set on thin layers of purified fat spread out on webs stretched on wooden frames. These were, in turn, piled up one on the other and contained inside an enclosed space, then heated. Different temperatures could produce various results. All this took ten to twelve weeks of work, during which the petals were replaced at least fifty times. This degree of processing quickly became semi-industrial and took place in factories, where a ton of rose petals could be handled by five or six women in charge of some eight hundred frames. This technique can still be seen in the family establishments of the main perfumers of Grasse: Fragonard, Galimard, and Molinard, among others. As of 1845, the principal perfumers were treating more than 200 tons of flowers annually. In 1912, this figure went beyond 3,000. So it was that, thanks to *enfleurage*, the production of rose essence became semi-industrial and the entire town was transformed. All sorts of secondary manufacturing sprang up to provide bottling, packaging, labeling, and so on. Another major change occurred in the late the nineteenth century, when solvents were introduced and extraction became dominated by the use of chemical techniques of ever greater complexity. Today, Grasse has kept up a small-scale production highly appreciated for its fine quality, but the centers of the perfume industry have spread worldwide, catering to clients satisfied with less-refined products.

As for gastronomy, rose petals have been eaten since Roman times at the very least. The Roman gastronome Apicius, author of a legendary cookbook, includes several rose recipes. Rose water was an important ingredient in the cuisine of the Popes in Avignon in the fourteenth century. The sixteenth-century Provençal prophet and cook Nostradamus, besides using violets and borage, invented jams using the petals of Provins and damask roses. Jacques Chibois adds rose water to certain sauces as well as a rose syrup imported from Lebanon for some of his desserts, as is the custom in many Arab countries. He uses rose petals to decorate salads or even as a main ingredient, appreciating not only their color but also a texture not unlike that of endive. He also likes the slightly acid taste of rose petals as a complement to many sauces, but he recommends using only pastel colors so as to avoid a jarring note in the presentation. A dish with roses unites, in the best Mediterranean tradition, flavor, perfume, and pleasure for the eye.

Following page:
Rose petals melt in
the mouth.

Grasse-style roses
with wild strawberries and pistachios

For 4 servings:
— For the pistachio sponge cake: 3 egg whites, 7 tablespoons granulated sugar, ¾ cup powdered sugar, 2 ounces (½ cup) ground almonds, 1 ounce (¼ cup) ground pistachios
— For the rose syrup: ¾ cup mineral water, ½ cup granulated sugar, ½ teaspoon cornstarch, 3 tablespoons rose water
— For the mascarpone cream: ½ cup whipping cream, 2 egg yolks, 2 tablespoons granulated sugar, ½ cup mascarpone cream
— For the crystallized rose petals: 1 egg white, 30 untreated rose petals, 2 tablespoons granulated sugar
— For the presentation: 1 pint (1½ to 2 cups) wild strawberries, 1 tablespoon coarsely chopped pistachios, a few untreated rose petals.

For the pistachio sponge cake

Preheat the oven to 350°F. Combine the egg whites and sugar, and whip to stiff peaks. Sift the powdered sugar, ground almonds, and ground pistachios together to remove any lumps. Pour the sifted dry ingredients into a mixing bowl and delicately fold in the egg whites. Place 4 metal pastry rings (about 4½-inch diameter) on a baking sheet covered with parchment or a silicone sheet. Spoon a thin layer (about ⅜-inch) of the batter into each ring. Bake for 10 about minutes, do not over bake. Remove the rings and let cool.

The rose syrup

Bring the mineral water and sugar to a boil in a saucepan. Dissolve the cornstarch in the rose water, pour into the sugar syrup and bring to a boil, stirring constantly. Refrigerate in a covered container until using.

The mascarpone cream

Beat the whipping cream to soft peaks. Whisk the egg yolks and the sugar together for about 5 minutes until the mixture becomes thick and foamy. Whisk the mascarpone cream in a bowl, then delicately fold in the egg yolk mixture and the whipped cream. Refrigerate for 1 hour.

Crystalized rose petals

Whisk the egg white briefly. Dip the rose petals in the egg whites, sprinkle with the sugar, a little at a time, shaking off any excess. Place the rose petals on a sheet of baking parchment and let dry.

Presentation

In the center of each serving plate, place a round of the pistachio sponge cake, top with a dome of the mascarpone cream leaving an outside rim of about ¼ inch. Arrange the wild strawberries, stem-side down, in a crown around the mascarpone cream, anchoring them firmly in the sponge cake. Arrange a few crystallized rose petals, upright, between cream and strawberries, and sprinkle with the chopped pistachios. Spoon a ribbon of the rose syrup around and decorate with the rose petals.

* IF GROUND ALMONDS AND PISTACHIOS ARE NOT AVAILABLE, *a home version can be made by grinding blanched, dried almonds or pistachios in a food processor. Grind with quick pulses of the processor until reduced to a fine powder (being careful not to grind too much or the mixture will turn into an oily paste). Sift through a fine sieve before using.*

CHEF'S NOTE

It is essential here to use garden roses, wonderfully fragrant and untreated.

The Chef's Advice

COOKING WITH FLOWERS

Certain flowers add flavor, others improve the presentation of a dish and still others add aroma. In my cooking, I frequently use roses, rosemary flowers, and jasmine. The taste of flowers is always very delicate. On the other hand, a branch or sprig of rosemary has a certain intensity, a powerful punch not found in its flowers, which are much more subtle. Sprinkling flowers on a salad or adding them, just before serving, to a sauce gives a very pleasant result, not only for the eyes, but for the taste, because their flavor is milder and less aggressive than the plants from which they bloom. Keep in mind that flowers have very volatile essences, so it is best to add them at the end of any preparation and to serve the dish quickly afterward.

I have a lot of fun with flowers. They add a certain fantasy, they light up a dish and make it more beautiful, and in addition, they add flavor. Many flowers are edible and their use in cooking is not recent, they have been employed forever. Despite this, as when cooking with mushrooms, it is important to know what you are doing and to verify that the flowers you are using are not toxic. Luckily, the choice of edible varieties is so vast (marigolds, borage, etc), that you should have no problem finding the best flowers for garnishing your dishes.

SALAGON

ANCIENT GARDENS FOR MODERN TIMES

Above:
The famous Lablab
bean, grown in Europe
since ancient times.

Right:
Ethnobotanists at
Salagon celebrate
biodiversity worldwide
while protecting local
varieties.

THE PRIORY OF SALAGON is situated in the alps of northern Provence, near the village of Mane and the town of Forcalquier. Its medieval buildings stand in the midst of a plain surrounded by mountains, on land which was farmed in Gallo-Roman times and Christianized towards the end of the Roman Empire. There are still traces here of an early Christian cemetery and a basilica built between the fifth and seventh centuries. The Benedictine church, still present with its beautiful carved portal, dates from the twelfth century. A manor house from the sixteenth century and outbuildings from various eras complete the picture today.

Since 1981, this complex has housed the Ethnological Museum of Haute-Provence. Since 2000, it has been managed by the depart-mental government and carries on a variety of activities besides bio-ethnological research: exhibits, a lending library, meetings and conventions, workshops, activities for children and school groups, and seasonal festivals. This ancient site has always been open to the world, a crossroads both in time and in space. Now it boasts four gardens that surround the Priory, each one associated with a different point of the compass. The South Garden was created first, in 1985. It illustrates the research on regional flora conducted by renowned botanist Pierre Lieutaghi, who still provides scientific supervision of all the gardens. On this spot where monks once grew vegetables, he planted specimens of all the useful plants found on farmland in the Haute-Provence, including those from abandoned fields. An ancient pear tree adds character to the scene. Next came the North Garden, a checkerboard patterning in the spirit of monastery gardens, presenting more than 300 species. Designers Michel Racine and Alain Richert planned this garden, while botanists Pierre Lieutaghi and Dorothy Dore chose and planted the varieties, aided by the Gairaut nursery, specialists in heirloom collections. Inside its walls, an old well, a walnut tree, and a number of shrubs have been preserved from older plantings set around a central axis leading to a

fountain. Two irregular beds on each side contain plants organized by theme: edible, medicinal, magical, and ornamental. Without pretending to be a historic reconstitution, this garden is an attractive presentation of plants commonly grown in medieval times. Some are now rare in the region: the Florentine black cabbage, sea kale, and the azerolle. Others, although ancient, have recently become popular again: atriplex, purslane, borage, different kinds of amaranthus, and rocket. The third garden, to the east, was planted to extend a temporary exhibit on herbs and aromatics. It is today a vast parterre displaying rich collections of mints, sages, artemisias, and many ombelliferous plants (of the Queen Anne's Lace family). These three gardens were created over the years for different purposes in existing spaces, in harmony with the historic buildings, without any modification of the landscape or surrounding views. They each have a different mood and are educational in pleasing and attractive ways.

The fourth, westerly garden is called the Garden of Modern Times and was begun in 1998. Once again, Pierre Lieutaghi provided its

philosophical underpinnings but the Parisian landscape architecture studio, Bruel-Delmar, designed the layout in conjunction with the managing council. The elegant lines of the church's west façade inspired the overall plan, as did the site itself with its farming history and dramatic surrounding landscapes. Imagined on a large scale, open and visible from everywhere, these gardens spread out in strong contrast to the other, more intimate parts of the domain. They contain a great variety of plantings. In a northwest corner is a display of a typical ecosystem of the area, showing the most common associations as they appear in nature in the wet or dry areas, in the habitat of the common white oak (*Quercus pubescens*). The large, central part takes visitors around the world on a tour of useful plants in modern times: the civilizing plants (those which permitted the discovery of new techniques for domestic or industrial use); food plants including medicinal aromatics, of which 80% were discovered through their use for food; and finally those which have had throughout the ages a symbolic or magic function. The beds are laid out in three long strips repre-senting Europe, Asia, and the Americas. Each contains a long pool of water ending in a pergola. The many food plants imported into Europe from the Americas at the time of the Renaissance stand here in good stead, including tomatoes and potatoes. The average winter temperatures at Salagon are just a bit too low for growing olive trees (averaging –7°C with occasional lows of –12°C). Only truly hardy plants can survive here so tender exotics must be grown as annuals.

In 1980, Pierre Lieutaghi had already summed up his conception of the ideal garden. "It teaches us partnership with the world of plants and introduces us to both their earthly and cosmic dimensions. It is a school for understanding the world around us." Faithful to that spirit, the different gardens of Salagon, each with its own character, unite the medieval idea of *harmonia mundi* with the experiences of a new global age.

Above:
Japanese knotweed, introduced into France in the nine-teenth century, now a roadside fixture.

Right:
The Garden of Modern Times opposite the twelfth-century portal.

Sautéed veal liver
with buckwheat, red lentils, verbena, lemongrass, and cilantro sauce

FOR 4 SERVINGS:
— FOR THE VEAL LIVER: 4 SLICES VEAL LIVER (EACH TRIMMED TO A NEAT, ½-INCH-THICK RECTANGLE), ½ TABLESPOON OLIVE OIL, 1 TABLESPOON SHERRY VINEGAR
— FOR THE BUCKWHEAT: 2 TABLESPOONS OLIVE OIL, 1 CUP BUCKWHEAT GROATS OR KASHA, SALT, PEPPER, 2 TEASPOONS UNSALTED BUTTER.
— FOR THE SAUCE: 1 OUNCE COOKED RED BEET, 1 PINCH POWDERED POULTRY BOUILLON, ½ CUP (3½ OUNCES) RED LENTILS, SALT, PEPPER, 12 LEAVES FRESH LEMON VERBENA, 2 TEASPOONS UNSALTED BUTTER, A FEW DROPS LEMON JUICE, 1 TABLESPOON OLIVE OIL, 1 TABLESPOON PINE NUTS, 5 LEAVES LEMONGRASS, 5 LEAVES CILANTRO
— FOR THE PRESENTATION: FRESHLY GROUND PEPPER, A FEW LEAVES LEMON VERBENA OR LEMONGRASS

The veal livers

Sear the liver quickly on both sides in the oil in a nonstick skillet. When nicely browned, deglaze the pan with Sherry vinegar. Transfer the liver to a rack, cover with aluminum foil and let rest.

The buckwheat

Preheat the oven to 350°F. Heat the oil in a Dutch oven, add the buckwheat and sauté until well browned. Add 1¼ cups water, season with salt and pepper. Cover and bake in the oven until all of the liquid has evaporated. Remove from the oven, add the butter, and fluff with a fork to separate the grains.

The sauce

Dice the beet and place in a saucepan with ⅔ cup water and the powdered bouillon. Bring to a boil. Add the red lentils, season with salt and pepper, and cook for 2 to 5 minutes, testing for doneness (be very careful that they do not overcook). Remove from the heat. Drain the lentils, reserving their cooking liquid. Infuse the lemon verbena for 3 minutes in the hot lentil cooking liquid. Remove the lemon verbena, strain the cooking liquid, into a small saucepan and reduce for 2 minutes over low heat. Add the butter, lemon juice, and olive oil. Return the lentils to the sauce with the pine nuts. Just before serving, add the lemon grass and cilantro leaves.

Presentation

Spoon a tablespoon of buckwheat onto each serving place. Top with a slice of liver and a little of the herb and lentil garnish with its sauce. Spoon a ribbon of sauce over all and season with freshly ground pepper. Decorate with lemon verbena and lemon grass leaves.

CHEF'S NOTE

Choose veal liver of a pale color and small size. Sear it quickly in the skillet, then let it rest to allow the warmth to penetrate slowly to the center of the liver. Above all, do not dust it with flour before cooking.

The Chef's Advice

INFUSING SAUCES

It is important to understand, first of all, that we're talking about infusions here and not decoctions. In other words, we are not boiling something in a liquid, but we are simply letting something infuse its flavor into a liquid. However, the difference between the "classic" infusion in which a plant soaks in boiling water and my method, is that here, the plant infuses directly into a sauce without the hot water. The flavor produced is thus much more concentrated. A wide array of plants and aromatics can be used—fennel, lemon grass, rosemary, thyme—and this method is sure to accentuate the taste.

To make a lemongrass sauce, chop the lemongrass, then process or blend it to pulverize the cells of the leaves. Add the leaves immediately to the preprepared sauce base. Alternatively, the sauce can be poured directly over the chopped lemongrass, allowed to infuse briefly, and then strained.

For a rosemary sauce, chop the rosemary, add it to the sauce, then heat it gently, tasting frequently because the flavors infuse quickly. Stop infusing while the taste of rosemary is still fresh and clean, not too strong. Take care to preserve this freshness, because if the sauce boils, it will create what we call a decoction: the rosemary will lose its aroma and will take on an unpleasant hay-like taste.

This operation should be done very quickly, in barely a minute, then remove the sauce from the heat and strain quickly. Your sauces, infused in this way, will be enriched with the fresh taste of the plant, which is always very agreeable.

THE GARDENS OF SAINT-ANTOINE

Above:
A young olive tree
among the hundreds
in the garden.

THE BASTIDE SAINT-ANTOINE is typical of the eighteenth-century manor houses of Grasse. A thriving perfume industry at that time led the city to expand, and each new neighborhood had its own *bastide*. The one at Saint-Antoine overlooks fifteen acres of terraced hillside covered with hundreds of ancient olive trees, all with massive trunks and gnarled roots. When Jacques Chibois bought this estate in 1994, everything needed restoration. In his efforts, Chibois has been guided by the spirit of the Bastide's owner in the late nineteenth and early twentieth centuries: the legendary Riviera gardener John Taylor.

The story begins in 1834 when the English chancellor Lord Brougham settled in Cannes. Many of his friends followed suit and built huge villas on the surrounding hilltops. The French historian and writer Prosper Mérimée criticized their taste vehemently and objected to these "cardboard castles set on the peaks of our most beautiful mountains," which he judged as out of place as "paper flowers in the middle of a parterre!" Some years later, another writer, Guy de Maupassant, compared them to the eggs of huge birds laid in green settings. Architectural fashion at the time favored exoticism: Gothic, Moorish, or Italian styles intermingled in both the villas of the newcomers and their gardens. A leader among the settlers was an Anglican minister, Thomas Woolfield, to whom is attributed the importation of the eucalyptus (*E. globulus*) from Australia and a winter flowering tree commonly called mimosa (*Acacia dealbata*) in the region today. Woolfield also grew the first sweet potatoes, introduced from Jamaica. He spared no expense on his croquet lawns that were particularly admired by Queen Victoria herself. Finally, this enterprising man supplied all his friends with properties on which elaborate gardens had already been established, awaiting only the construction of a fine residence by the new purchaser. Little by little, Woolfield found himself absorbed by the real estate business. He needed help and got it from another of his imports, a

Above:
Bougainvillea and a
red-flowered trumpet
vine deck the facade.

22-year-old gardener from northern England. This was John Taylor, who in 1864 went on to found the Taylor Agency, still today one of the most prestigious of the region. When Taylor chose a property for himself, however, he rejected the elaborate white elephants rising behind Cannes. His preference went to an elegant but traditional manor house: the Bastide Saint Antoine, where natural grass full of wildflowers still replaces velvet expanses of English lawns.

Taylor was successful in many activities. He founded a bank in order to make loans to clients needing financing for their real estate purchases. He became a wine merchant and publisher of an English-language newsletter that was delivered three times a day to the best hotels, providing English visitors with both gossip and weather reports. He opened an English language library in Cannes, next door to his offices. He was British consul for decades, and his Bastide thus became a diplomatic residence. It was no doubt Taylor who first covered the façade of the building with ramblers and climbers, as was customary in England but not in Provence.

Still today a luxuriant purple bougainvillea ("floral lava," as the writer Colette called it) flowers almost year round. It intermingles with a lesser-known climber, a cerise-flowered trumpet vine (*Tecomaria capensis*). The fact that this less-than-hardy plant has survived here for decades proves that the Bastide enjoys a particularly mild microclimate.

Between Taylor's descendants and Jacques Chibois, there was only one other owner, who installed the discrete swimming pool one level below the house. Easily accessible, it enjoys a wonderful view but is hidden by hedges on the three other sides. A small, shady terrace across the way, among the camellias, now offers tables and chairs for the aperitif hour.

The Bastide gardens have kept the layout of the old farm gardens of the region with broad cobblestone paths meandering among the olive terraces. Part of the farm buildings have survived: a cistern, the cold frames for winter, a small greenhouse. The highly productive olive orchards are punctuated by massive black cypresses and surrounded in places with swaths of agapanthus, while an old well is garlanded with purple-flowered passion vine. Here is a carpet of bergenia, there the popular Riviera rambling rose Sénateur Lafollette reaching the top of an olive tree. Many paths are edged with oleander. Some chefs establish show gardens for their clients, but Jacques Chibois, of sound country stock, considers himself simply lucky to live surrounded by authentic countryside, a real treasure on the Riviera. He is developing some sections so he can experiment with citrus and a collection of table grapes, restoring the green house and the vegetable garden. But overall, the gardens will remain a timeless place for quiet walks. To ensure easy access to all the terraces and establish overall harmony, Chibois sought the advice of garden designer Jean Mus, famous for his work in Riviera gardens and himself a descendant of farmers and gardeners of Grasse. Mus sees in the gardens of Saint Antoine "a typical, peaceful country garden of the region." He admires their simplicity: a single main avenue, strongly delineated terracing and the olive tree as the keynote. "Simplicity" is one of the words Chibois uses frequently to describe his culinary ideal. As always, the garden is the portrait of its owner.

Red mullet
sautéed with mimosa flowers

For 4 servings :
— For the vegetables: 10 ½ ounces snow peas, salt, pepper
— For the sauce: 1 tablespoon unsalted butter, a few drops lemon juice, 1 pinch white ground cardamom, 1 pinch ground ginger, a few untreated mimosa flowers*
— For the red mullet: 4 red mullet (10½ ounces each), filleted, salt, pepper, 1 tablespoon olive oil, the juice of ½ lemon.
— For the presentation: 1½ tablespoons julienne of untreated lemon zest, mimosa flowers and snow peas

The vegetables

Cook the snow peas in a large saucepan of boiling salted water (1½ tablespoons salt for 1 quart water). When tender, plunge the peas into cold water and drain immediately. Set aside a dozen snow peas for the presentation and finely shred the remaining peas. Just before serving, reheat them in a saucepan with a few drops of water, salt, and pepper.

The sauce

Combine ½ cup water in a saucepan with the butter, lemon juice, cardamom, ginger, and the mimosa flowers (reserving about a dozen mimosa flowers for the presentation). Bring to a boil quickly; remove from the heat and strain the sauce through a fine sieve.

The red mullet

Season the red mullet with salt and pepper. Just before serving, heat the oil in a nonstick skillet and sear the fillets quickly, skin-side down, then turn and cook for about 2 more minutes or until cooked to taste. Drizzle the lemon juice over the fish at the end of the cooking.

Presentation

Arrange the snow peas on each plate with a little of the sauce, place the mullet on top, and spoon the sauce over. Decorate with the lemon zest, mimosa flowers, and snow peas.

* Mimosa flowers: *the bright little yellow balls of mimosa flowers add a special taste to this recipe. If they are not available, substitute other untreated flowers such as violets, cherry blossoms, acacia flowers, or rose petals.*

CHEF'S NOTE

Sear the red mullets quickly, then set them aside to finish cooking slowly. If overcooked, they become dry and insipid. Before cooking, use tweezers to remove any little bones on the edges of the fillets.

Ribbons of warm leeks
with truffles

For 4 servings: 6 leeks, 1¼ ounces black truffles, 5 tablespoons olive oil, 1 teaspoon lemon juice, salt, pepper.
— For the presentation: 1½ ounces purslane* greens

The leek ribbons

Trim the leeks, removing the roots and the dark green part of the leaves. Cut each into 6-inch lengths, then cut in half lengthwise, separate the leaves and rinse them thoroughly.

Cook the leek leaves for 5 minutes in a large pan of salted boiling water (1½ tablespoons salt to 1 quart water). When tender, plunge leeks into cold water; drain immediately. Set aside at room temperature. Leeks should remain slightly warm.

The truffle vinaigrette

Brush the truffle and rinse under running water. Peel it with a vegetable peeler, reserving the peelings. Slice the truffle thinly and set aside. Combine the olive oil, lemon juice, salt, pepper, and truffle peelings and process until the truffle peelings are finely chopped.

Presentation

Season the leek leaves with part of the truffle vinaigrette. Arrange them attractively in a ring on each serving plate. Rinse and dry the purslane leaves, divide them among the servings, and top with the truffle slices. Drizzle a little of the remaining truffle vinaigrette over each serving.

* Purslane, *called* pourpier *in French, is a salad green or pot herb with thick, fleshy leaves. If not available, substitute other greens such as lamb's lettuce.*

CHEF'S NOTE

It is best to choose young leeks that are not too large—they will be more tender.

JACQUES CHIBOIS

VISITS THE GARDENS OF VAL JOANIS

Above:
Ancient tools and
techniques.

Right:
The collection of
rare vegetables gives
onto the Val Joanis
vineyards.

VAL JOANIS IS A THRIVING WINE PROPERTY set on the southern slopes of the Luberon hills, north of Aix-en-Provence. In this secret valley, a three-tiered vegetable garden overlooks vineyards and olive orchards. Flowers and vegetables are planted here together in orderly rows, medicinal plants and herbs laid out at the foot of apple cordons. Red-, orange-, and yellow-ribbed chard rises among lettuce with bronze, golden, or apple-green leaves. Dozens of tomato varieties grow supported by bamboo stakes, their own rainbow colors set off by a hedge of mahonia (Oregon grape). This shrub is an unusual choice for a vegetable garden, but its tough foliage provides a solid mass year-round while changing tones throughout the season. It also has yellow flowers in summer and blue berries in winter. Along the east edge of the potager runs an extended pergola, saved from the ruins of a local château park. Its arches are decked with fragrant roses including the Banks, Bobbie Jones, Kiftsgate, and Madame Isaac Pereire varieties. The lower levels of the potager are given over to more flowering shrubs and fruit.

Val Joanis was named after a seventeenth-century owner, Jean de Joanis, secretary of Louis III, king of Naples. The Chancel family began restoring the domain in 1977. Jean-Louis Chancel planted some 200 acres of vines on these slopes where Romans vineyards prospered 2,000 years ago—but he had them all carefully regraded first. Cécile Chancel created the potager with the help of garden designer Tobie Loup de Viane, taking inspiration from eighteenth century models that were both ornamental and productive. Recently, a link to the vineyards was created with an avenue of mixed olive trees and cypresses, an elegant line laid out by Parisian designer Louis Benech.

Growing conditions are difficult here. The terrain is very limey (with a pH of 8.5), and at 280 meters above sea level, winters are cold and summers are hot. Cécile Chancel continues to experiment both in the

garden and in the kitchen. She created endless recipes for zucchini of every color and size until her children cried for mercy. Her eye guides her as much as her palate. She stopped using red basil, white eggplant, and yellow zucchini because she felt none of them look good on a plate. Above all, she cooks according to the season. She has help both in the garden and in the house ("We are often fourteen at table," she explains), but when the menu calls for tiny artichokes made into a "barigoule," she prepares the dish herself, even though her hands are blackened by the inevitable oxidation of the vegetables. Growing her produce and preparing it to eat are both very personal experiences for her.

When Jacques Chibois came to visit late one summer, he was moved by the profusion he discovered in the garden. This rustic intermingling of flowers, fruit, herbs, and vegetables reminded him of old-fashioned cottage gardens, although here the scale is vast and the layout formal. He admired Cécile Chancel's blending of heirloom vegetables with modern ones, local Mediterranean varieties with adapted exotics. "They look as if they had always been there," he observed. This

Above right:
Cabbage, peppers and
tomatoes grow between
the tool shed and a
mahonia hedge.

amazing variety set him imagining how he might use some of this and some of that in new ways. Flavor blends, he feels, can be directly inspired by the planting schemes of the garden. Above all, he takes his cue from the unpredictable results of the harvest, since the same vegetables rarely ripen together from one season to the next. Jacques Chibois recalls his good friend, garden designer Jean Mus, who also lives in Grasse. Jean said to him one day, "When I make a new garden, I sit for a long time on the spot and just look around me. Everything in a sense is already there, I just have to assemble it." A cook has even wider choices because he can begin over and over again. "A vegetable garden is constantly changing," Chibois observes. "This year the green beans are late and there are no apples." The possibilities are infinite.

Jacques Chibois appreciates the freshness and simplicity of Val Joanis's wines. The idea is to observe what is already there, then make the most of it with verve and originality. Thus does the gardener, the designer, but also of the vintner and the cook. Such a philosophy gives as much pleasure to the creators as to their admirers.

Poached peaches
with lemon verbena ice cream

For 4 servings:
— For the pastry curls: ⅓ pound (5¼ ounces) puff pastry, 4 tablespoons powdered sugar, 1½ tablespoons unsalted butter (for the baking sheet)
— For the verbena ice cream: 3¼ cups milk, 1 bunch fresh lemon verbena (or 1¼ ounces dried verbena leaves or lemongrass), ¼ cups cream, 1⅓ cups granulated sugar, 8 egg yolks
— For the peaches: 2 cups water, ½ cup granulated sugar, 5 leaves fresh lemon verbena, juice of 1 lemon, 4 large white peaches
— For the presentation: 1 bunch fresh lemon verbena, 10½ ounces (about 1¾ cups) raspberries, powdered sugar

The pastry curls

Preheat the oven to 400°F. Roll the puff pastry out to about 1/16 inch. Cut into thin strips about 6-inches long and dust both sides with powdered sugar. Twist the strips, place on a buttered baking sheet and cook in the hot oven until golden brown. Set aside.

Lemon verbena ice cream

Bring the milk to a boil. Add the verbena leaves, remove from the heat and let infuse for 25 minutes. Strain the milk, add the cream, and reheat. Whisk the sugar and egg yolks together in a bowl, stir in the warm milk/cream mixture gradually. Return the mixture to the saucepan and cook gently over low heat, stirring constantly with a wooden spoon. When the mixture thickens, remove from the heat and strain immediately into a chilled bowl. Let cool, then process in an ice cream machine.

The peaches

In a saucepan, bring the water and sugar to a boil. Remove from the heat, add the verbena and infuse for 8 minutes. Strain, discarding the verbena, and add the lemon juice to the syrup. Drop the whole peaches into boiling water for 2 minutes, then plunge immediately into ice water. Drain the peaches, peel and cut in half, removing the pit. Place peaches in the syrup and simmer for 10 to 12 minutes over low heat. Remove from the heat and let cool.

Presentation

Chop some lemon verbena leaves. Cut the peaches in quarters and arrange them on the serving plates. Place a scoop of verbena ice cream in the center, decorate with raspberries. Spoon a little of the peach syrup over all and top with chopped verbena leaves. Stand the puff pastry curls in the ice cream. Garnish with whole verbena leaves and sprinkle with powdered sugar.

CHEF'S NOTE

This aromatic and flavorful dessert merits a bubbly accompaniment such as a bottle of sparkling Gaillac Mousseux 1995 from the Long-Pech domaine. Nonetheless, if at the end of a summer meal you feel like prolonging the pleasure of the wine that accompanied lunch, don't hesitate to continue serving a Tavel 1998 from the domain Mordorée.

Crisp raspberry
millefeuille

For 4 servings:
— For the raspberry sauce: 5 ounces (about 1 cup) raspberries, ⅔ cup granulated sugar, a few drops lemon juice
— For the lemon grass jelly: ⅓ cup granulated sugar, 10 trimmed lemongrass leaves, 1 tablespoon grated zest of untreated lemon, ½ vanilla bean, 1½ tablespoons unflavored gelatin (one and one-half 1/4-ounce envelopes) or 6 sheets gelatin, a few drops lemon juice
— For the "sugar leaves": 1 cup, 2⅔ cups granulated sugar, 5 tablespoons glucose*
— For the presentation: 9 ounces (about 1⅓ cups) raspberries, lemongrass leaves

The raspberry sauce

Process the raspberries, sugar and lemon juice to a purée. Strain and refrigerate, covered, until using.

Lemon grass jelly

In a saucepan, boil the sugar with 1 cup water. Add the lemongrass leaves, lemon zest and ½ vanilla bean, split open lengthwise. Remove from the heat and let infuse for 8 minutes. Strain the syrup through a fine sieve, setting aside a small amount for the presentation. Soften the gelatin in two tablespoons cold water, then stir it into the warm syrup along with the lemon juice. Pour this mixture in a thin, even layer (about ¼-inch thick) onto a rimmed-baking sheet covered with plastic film, and let cool. Refrigerate until set, about an hour.

Sugar Leaves

Preheat the oven to 350°F. Boil the mineral water, sugar, and glucose in a saucepan and cook the syrup to the hard-crack stage (about 300°F), testing the temperature with a sugar thermometer. Plunge the bottom of the saucepan into a bowl of ice water to quickly stop the cooking. Immediately, pour the syrup onto a baking sheet lined with a silicone sheet and let cool.

Use a rolling pin to break up and crush the cooled sugar, reducing it to a fine powder. Sift the powder to separate out the large pieces, and continue to roll, crush and sift them in the same manner. Sprinkle this sugar powder over the silicone-lined baking sheet and place in the pre-heated oven for about 30 seconds, just long enough to melt the sugar. Remove from the oven, quickly cut into 2-inch by 5-inch rectangles using a large knife. (These rectangles are extremely fragile. Handle carefully to prevent them from breaking.) Let cool and set aside in a dry place.

Presentation

Line up 10 raspberries (2 lines of 5) in the center of each serving plate. Top with a sugar rectangle, then with a rectangle of the same size of lemon grass jelly. Top with 8 raspberries and another rectangle of sugar. Pour a ribbon of the reserved lemongrass syrup around each serving, sprinkle with a few drops of the raspberry sauce, garnish with lemon-grass and serve immediately.

* GLUCOSE, *used to prevent crystallization, is found in pharmacies and in some specialty baking stores. If not available, increase the amount of sugar by 2 tablespoons and frequently brush the sides of the pan with cold water as the sugar cooks.*

CHEF'S NOTE

If fresh lemongrass is not available, fresh mint or the leaves of fresh lemon verbena can be substituted. Assemble the millefeuille *just before serving, since the sugar leaves soften and melt in contact with the humidity of the fruit and jelly.*

The Chef's Advice

PICKING AND KEEPING FRUITS

It's preferable to pick fruits—such as apples, peaches, plums, apricots—when they are not yet completely ripe and to let them ripen, very slowly, in a cool place. Fruits plucked at maximum maturity are often bruised and, in addition, a fully ripened fruit will not keep for very long once picked. It is the same as for flowers that are cut when they just begin to open so that they can bloom fully in the house. After the picking, it is up to you to handle the ripening.

In the past, when we picked apples in the country we were always careful not to choose the ripest fruits and then to spread them out on racks in the cellar away from the light, but in a well ventilated place. This way, depending upon the variety of the apple, we could keep them for as long as five to six months. But if the ripening was already too advanced when they were picked, the apples couldn't be kept for more than three weeks.

In fact, slowing down the maturing process at the right moment doesn't change the quality of the fruit. This doesn't mean, however, picking a fruit when it is still green.

Grapes are picked early to obtain a certain taste, later for another taste, or even later when we want them to develop the pourriture noble or noble rot necessary for producing a sauternes or a muscat wine.

We pick everything at different stages of maturity depending upon what we want to create with them. It all comes down to a question of managing time.

Meringue leaves
layered with lemon sorbet, mandarin orange sorbet and candied olives

For 4 servings:
— For the meringue leaves: 2 egg whites, ¼ cup granulated sugar
— For the Mandarin* orange marmalade: 1⅓ cups granulated sugar, 4 mandarin oranges
— For the amaretto cream: 1 cup whipping cream, 2 tablespoons powdered sugar, 1½ tablespoons amaretto (almond liqueur)
— For the candied olives: 8 black olives (not pitted), 1 cup granulated sugar
— For the mandarin* orange sorbet: 1 cup fresh-squeezed mandarin orange juice (with the pulp), 2 cups granulated sugar, grated zest of 2 mandarin oranges, 3¼ cups mineral water
— For the lemon sorbet: 1 cup fresh-squeezed lemon juice (with the pulp), 2 cups granulated sugar, grated zest of 2 lemons, 3¼ cups mineral water
— For the vanilla olive oil: ½ cup olive oil, 2 vanilla beans
— For the lemon cream: 1 package (2⅔ ounces) instant vanilla pudding mix, 1 tablespoon limoncello (lemon liqueur), ½ cup whipping cream
— For the presentation: a few olive leaves

The meringue leaves

Preheat the oven to 250° F. Combine the egg whites and sugar in a large bowl. Hold over a saucepan of boiling water (or in a double boiler), whisking and cooking until stiff peaks form on the end of the whisk when lifted out of the bowl. Cut a stencil out of clean cardboard in the form of a teardrop about 4 inches long. Cover a baking sheet with baking parchment and, using the stencil, spread the meringue mixture evenly, about ⅛-inch thick, to form 8 teardrops. Cook in the preheated oven until ivory-colored and dry to the touch, about 1 hour. Remove the teardrops delicately from the parchment and store in a dry place.

The Mandarin orange marmalade

In a saucepan, boil 1 cup water with the sugar. Peel the Mandarins, remove any seeds, separate the segments, prick each with a toothpick and let simmer slowly in the syrup over very low heat for about an hour. Remove from the heat and let cool. Remove the Mandarin segments from the syrup and process to a purée, adding a little additional syrup if necessary. Keep cool.

The amaretto cream

Whip the cream until soft peaks form, fold in the powdered sugar and the amaretto. Chill.

The candied olives

Drop the black olives into a saucepan of cold water and bring to a boil. Strain immediately, and repeat this operation four times to remove the natural bitterness of the olives. Drain the olives. In a saucepan, boil 1 cup water with the sugar. Add the olives, reduce the heat, and simmer gently over very low heat for 1 hour.

The mandarin sorbet

In a saucepan, heat together the Mandarin juice and pulp, sugar, zest, and mineral water. Let infuse for 1 hour. Process in a sorbet machine. Store in the freezer.

The lemon sorbet

In a saucepan, combine the lemon juice and pulp, sugar, zest, and warm with the mineral water. Let infuse for 1 hour. Process in a sorbet machine. Store in the freezer.

The vanilla olive oil

Heat the olive oil to 175°F in a saucepan (using a frying thermometer). Split the vanilla beans in half lengthwise, scrape out the beans with the tip of a paring knife, and add them to the oil. Let infuse, off the heat, for 1 hour. Set aside.

The lemon cream

Prepare the pudding following package instructions and stir in the lemoncello. Strain into a bowl and let cool to room temperature. Whip the cream to soft peaks and fold into the pudding mixture.

Presentation

Place a dot of the lemon cream on each serving plate (to hold meringue in place) and place a meringue teardrop on top. Using a pastry bag fitted with a medium plain tip, pipe a border of lemon cream around each meringue teardrop. Using a soup spoon, form smooth oval scoops of lemon sorbet and place them on each meringue. Top with a second meringue teardrop. On the side, form a 2-inch circle of amaretto cream, top with 1 teaspoon Mandarin marmalade and 2 candied olives. Place an oval scoop of Mandarin sorbet on the amaretto cream. Delicately spoon a ribbon of the vanilla olive oil around, and decorate with olive leaves.

* Tangerines and clementines are varieties of Mandarin orange. Both work well in this recipe.

CHEF'S NOTE

Soak the gelatin in a little cold water for 3 to 5 minutes. This allows it to soften and swell without melting so that it will dissolve evenly when heated. If using gelatin leaves, soak them a little longer and squeeze out excess water before adding them to a preparation.

The Chef's Advice

FRUIT SORBETS

I never make syrups for fruit sorbets, but use only the sweetened fruit pulp with a touch of lemon juice. All of my sorbets are natural.

For a lemon sorbet, when you squeeze the fruit, let the juice run directly onto the sugar. This way, you immediately stop the fermentation and keep the clean taste of fresh lemon. If fruit juice is allowed to sit after being squeezed, even for as little as two minutes before preparing the sorbet, this can produce an unpleasant taste of oxidation similar to that found in artificially flavored beverages. In fact, lemon juice should always be pressed directly onto foods, regardless of what you are making.

To make a sorbet, sweeten the fruit to your taste, always add a drop of lemon juice, then turn or freeze it right away in the sorbet machine. In this way, the taste of fresh fruit is preserved. In addition, it is important to serve the sorbet as quickly as possible after it is made, before it hardens. If you want to keep a sorbet, you'll need to add chemical products that prevent it from hardening in the freezer and I don't recommend this. In a pinch, if the sorbet isn't served immediately, let it melt in the refrigerator at around 20 degrees, then turn it in the sorbet machine a second time just before serving. With this method, the taste won't be as good as for a freshly made sorbet.

The best sorbet is the one that you prepare shortly before a meal, or, ideally, during the first part of the dinner, so that it can be served five or ten minutes after coming out of the machine.

FIG FANATICS

We enjoy this fruit thanks to the secret loves of a helpful insect.

FOOD LOVERS THROUGHOUT HISTORY HAVE GLORIFIED FIGS. Jean-Baptiste de La Quintinie, gardener to the Sun King Louis XIV, was unequivocal. "A well-ripened fig is the best of all tree-grown fruit I have ever eaten, and most connoisseurs find them as delicious as I do." In the gardens at Versailles, La Quintinie grew figs espaliered against protecting walls. This method was favored for centuries in northern France, especially in the Parisian suburb of Argenteuil. But nineteenth-century novelist Alexandre Dumas, another famous gastronome, had very definite opinions about that. "In spite of everyone's high regard for Argenteuil figs, I insist that good figs can only be grown in the South," he wrote. Dumas was familiar with the many fine varieties which had already been developed in Mediterranean France. Indeed, as early as 1600, the southern agronomist Olivier de Serres recommended a wide range of figs, a fruit he, too, held in high esteem: "The goodness of a fig cannot be disputed, however divided opinion may be on other fruit. Figs and grapes, by universal acclaim, are the best of all. There are white, black, smoky, grey, tan, and green ones; big, medium-sized, and small; early and late ripening; of diverse and precious flavors." The varieties he cited so long ago is still very evocative: "partridge eye, figs of mercy, squeaky, ruddy, thick-skinned, angelic . . ."

The fig tree thrives in Mediterranean climates because it freezes at temperatures of less than -12°C. But even in this region, growing figs commercially poses real problems. Productive trees may bear over a long period of time. The crop is thus extended, but picking has to be done daily, as the fresh fruit does not store well. Luckily, there are growers who use small, old-fashioned farming methods, preserving techniques from the past. In Solliès-Pont in the Var department east of Marseille, producers have obtained a government label for a local variety to justify the higher prices such methods involve. Pierre Baud, on his farm near the Mont Ventoux north of Avignon, sells a dozen

varieties of fig wholesale and twenty more to private clients. His farm is also a nursery. His collection of rootstocks is vast, enriched yearly thanks to his travels to Morocco, the U.S.A., southern Italy, etc. Visitors come, taste, and take away a tree of the variety they like best. However, Baud forewarns customers that soil characteristics can make a big difference to flavor with figs. Everyone gets individual advice.

Another "fig fanatic," Francis Honoré, grows some 150 different varieties on twenty-five acres south of Avignon, in the Alpilles region. With his wife Jacqueline and their children, Philippe and Christine, he has been round the world seeking out the tastiest varieties, bringing samples home from South Africa, the U.S.A., Japan, India, and Brazil. The Honorés grow both the kind that bears twice (in July and in September) and the kind that produces continuously for two months in autumn. Jacqueline has become a specialist in preserves: jam, compote, chutney, syrup, and even a nectar that can be drunk as is, added to mixed drinks or used—as was already done by Roman cooks—to enrich sauces. The family sells three varieties of fresh fig: the *dauphine*, the *Caromb black*, and the *bourjasotte*. Francis also prepares his figs spread in an open fan shape, half-dried in the Provencal sunshine.

The fig tree is beautiful, "a perfection," says poet Francis Ponge, who admires its trunk, which he

MOUGINS (Alpes-M⁽ᵉˢ⁾). - Séchage des figues

perceives as "animal and mineral at the same time, smooth and dull." It is also mysterious: the fig's life cycle has intrigued observers over the centuries, once they discovered its unique method of pollinization. There are male and female trees, and what we call fruit are in fact, in both sexes, fleshy envelopes containing hundreds of flowers, all internal. In the male tree (called a *caprifiguier*) these remain dry and inedible. How then can fertilization take place? Wedlock is consummated thanks to a small wasp-like messenger called the "blastophage" (*Blastophaga psenes*). The insect's eggs are laid in the male figs and its offspring later emerge, covered with pollen. Some insects go towards a female fig tree, enter into its "fruit" and thus fertilize its internal flowers, which then mature, allowing the fig to ripen while the insect disappears. Other insects find another male fig tree and thus continue their own life cycle. In the first case, the insect serves the fruit; in the second, the fruit serves the insect. Entry in both cases is through the small cavity in the bottom of the "fruit." When the female figs are ready to eat, a drop of honey appears at this same spot.

Such secrets inspire poetry even among the growers. Francis Honoré says passionately, "Figs are for me a journey of initiation. The fig tree is Mediterranean in its very essence: fragile, quick-tempered, whole-hearted. It deserves as much loyalty as a wife and children." Among literary fig fanatics, Francis Ponge, always the bard of the senses, elevates the fig to the rank of "materialist consolation," while Provencal poet René Char attributes to the fruit he admires these words: "My appearance is defiance, but my depths are friendship." Thanks to the enthusiasm of producers like these, more and more people are making friends with figs.

Watermelon granité
with hibiscus flowers and fresh figs

For 4 servings:
— For the ice: ⅔ cup mineral water, ½ cup granulated sugar, 3 tablespoons untreated hibiscus flowers, 10½ ounces watermelon pulp, seeds removed
— For the presentation: 16 figs, a few hibiscus flowers

The granité or ice

In a saucepan, bring the mineral water and sugar to a boil. Add the hibiscus flowers and let infuse. Simmer for 6 to 8 minutes over low heat. Strain and let cool. Combine the hibiscus syrup with the watermelon pulp and process to a purée. Taste for sweetness, and add sugar if necessary. Pour the mixture in a ⅔-inch thick layer in a shallow container, and place in the freezer to harden. Scrape the surface of the ice from time to time with a fork to form a coarse-grained *granité*. Store in the freezer until just before serving.

Presentation

Rinse and halve the figs. Arrange them in the center of the serving plates. Spoon the granité on top. Decorate with the hibiscus flowers.

CHEF'S NOTE

It is essential to place the serving dishes in the freezer several hours before serving.

TOMATOES AND EGGPLANTS
REVOLUTIONARY VEGETABLES

TOMATOES AND EGGPLANTS seem essential to any mediterranean cuisine, but Provence only discovered them in the sixteenth century! The tomato was brought back from the Americas by the Conquistadors, along with squash, pumpkin, sweet corn, string beans, and green beans. Eggplant took a different route: from India to Spain, thanks to the Moors. Later introduced into Italy, it came to Provence at roughly the same time as the tomato. Both vegetables were regarded with great suspicion for a long time. Tomato leaves were known to be poisonous and eggplant was first called *mala insana* or "the mad apple" for its supposed effects on the human brain. Nevertheless, these two vegetables were destined to transform, little by little, all the cooking habits of Mediterranean France. So the culinary traditions that seem most ancient, local, rooted, and unchanged can be, in fact, relatively recent and involved travel across several continents.

A further 150 years passed before these two vegetables found their way to Paris. Their discovery by northerners was one of the minor but most unexpected results of the French Revolution of 1789. By this time in Provence, the tomato had become firmly established as a "working-class food that should be price controlled" (as cited in *Histoire des recettes de Provence*, by Simone Martin Villevieille). But in Paris, as late as 1804, in the *Almanach des gourmands*, gastronome Grimod de la Reynière has this to say of the tomato: "Fruit or vegetable as you wish [. . .], transplanted to Languedoc and Provence, it was almost unknown in Paris fifteen years ago. It was the deluge of Paris by southerners that brought tomatoes to the capital and got them acclimatized here. Almost all of the southerners got rich (because they were smart enough to stick together and help each other, in common cause). First very expensive, the tomato has now become ordinary and in this past year we see them arriving at the wholesale market by the basketful . . ." Apparently, it was the 500 delegates from Marseille, up from the South to attend the festivities of the National Federation on

Tomatoes and eggplants are relative newcomers to the gardens and tables of Provence.

July 14, 1790, who first demanded tomatoes during their stay in Paris. But choice Parisian connoisseurs had already encountered this exotic produce. According to historians Patrick and Lindsay Mikanovksi in their book *Tomato*, "the head cook of a princely house in Paris had published a recipe book containing four pages of tomato recipes" as early as 1750. The seed merchants Vilmorin-Andrieux cited the tomato in their catalogue as of 1778, at a time when they were also trying to promote potatoes. Diderot mentioned tomatoes also in his *Encyclopédie* and tomato sauce was hesitantly mentioned in an almanac in 1783. Still, it can be said that the specialists and scientists were just beginning to explore its possibilities when the enthusiasm of the Marseille crowd brought it to the attention of the public at large—and to the market gardeners.

It is interesting to note that the tomato met a similar fate in the United States. At a time when Thomas Jefferson was growing and admiring them in Virginia, the North still considered them highly dangerous. As late as 1840, in New Jersey, a courageous colonel by the name of Robert Gibbon won fame by his death-defying feat of . . . eating a raw tomato in public!

As for eggplant, the same writer Grimod mentions it (also in 1804) as another Mediterranean vegetable still "rather rare in Paris." A restaurant called the *Frères provençaux* (Provencal brothers)

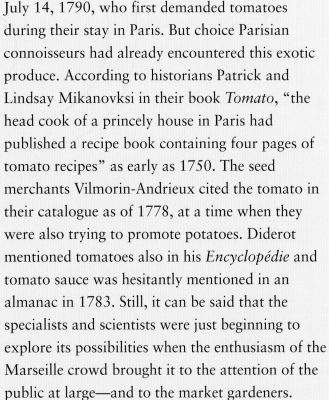

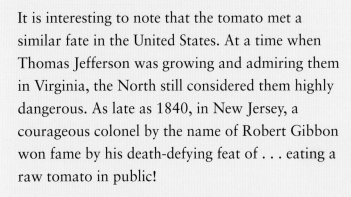

Fruit entier.

Fruit coupé.

is credited with having launched a fashion for eggplant in Paris around 1790, listing it on their menu as "grilled." This establishment was first founded in 1786 by three brothers-in-law from the Durance Valley (north of Aix). They first encountered great success at the Palais-Royal, a popular and somewhat shady meeting place in those days. Other southern specialties were also introduced: *cod brandade*, aioli, and bouillabaisse. Robespierre dined in this restaurant and later Bonaparte, though these patrons attest more to its popularity than to its quality. The poet Alfred de Musset used to organize bohemian parties there around 1830. Later on, it became a respectable and noteworthy table, the setting for scenes in the novels of Balzac and Flaubert. But in 1873, only four years before it closed for good, George Sand relates that she had "a very bad meal" there.

Food historian Jean-Paul Aron points out that the enterprising owners of the Frères Provence launched the fashion for regional food in Paris in the early days of the Revolution. After 1793, however, they were obliged to conform to the Jacobin, or centralizing, political faction. For the next eighty years, their menus avoided anything southern, with the occasional exceptions of bouillabaisse and salt cod with aïoli. The centralization of French political and social life in Paris increased throughout the nineteenth century and as a result, regional cuisines all but disappeared from Parisian restaurants.

Jacques Chibois likes to remember that tomatoes and eggplants are, botanically speaking, fruit, and can be treated as such. He prepares them in savory sauces, salads, and main dishes but also as sorbet, ice cream, and pastry. He even candies them in the manner much appreciated in Greek and Turkish cuisine. Along with Moroccan food, these exotic traditions inspire in him great admiration and often encourage his own inventions. Thus these vegetables, already so well-traveled, now participate in new, pan-Mediterranean exchanges.

Roast loin of veal
with capers, eggplant, and lemon

For 4 servings:
— For the veal loin: 1¼ pounds veal loin cut into 4 squares (each ¾ inch thick), salt, pepper, 1 tablespoon olive oil
— For the sauce: 2 small onions, 1 clove garlic, 1 carrot, 1 small branch celery, 3 ounces veal trimmings or veal breast, salt, pepper, 1 tablespoon olive oil, 3 tablespoons dry white wine, 1 bouquet garni (composed of a thyme sprig, a bay leaf, and a few sprigs parsley), 2 tablespoons chopped cooked red beet, 1 tablespoon chopped fresh tomato, 1 pinch ground cinnamon, 1 pinch grated nutmeg, a few slices dried cèpe mushrooms, 1½ tablespoons softened unsalted butter, a few drops lemon juice, 2 tablespoons small capers
— For the vegetables: 3 small eggplants, 4 cups (1 quart) peanut oil or other frying oil, salt, pepper, 1½ tablespoons butter, 1 pinch zest of untreated lemon, 1 pinch ground cumin

The veal loin

Season the veal with salt and pepper. Heat the oil in a nonstick skillet and sear the meat quickly on both sides over high heat. Remove from the skillet, place on a rack, cover with aluminum foil, and let rest in a warm oven (turned off). Just before serving, reheat the veal for a few minutes in the oven and cut into thick, diagonal slices.

The sauce

Peel and chop the onion, garlic, and carrot. Chop the celery. Cut the veal trimmings or breast into small pieces, season with salt and pepper, and brown in the olive oil in a Dutch oven. Add the onions, garlic, carrot, and celery. Sauté until well browned, then deglaze with the white wine. Add the bouquet garni, the beet, tomato, cinnamon, nutmeg and dried cèpes.

Stir in 1 cup water and cook for 20 minutes over low heat. Strain through a fine sieve, pressing the solids with a spoon to squeeze out all the juices. In a saucepan, reduce the liquid over low heat to about ½ cup. Whisk in the butter quickly, season with salt and pepper. Add the lemon juice. Just before serving reheat the sauce and add the capers.

The vegetables

Rinse the eggplant. Cut one of them into slices of about ¼-inch thick by 3 inches long (3 slices per person). Deep-fry the slices in the hot peanut oil until lightly browned. Remove and drain on absorbent paper. Season with salt and pepper.

Peel the remaining eggplants reserving the skin. Cut the skin in thin, even strips, and dice the flesh into cubes. Soak the skin and the flesh in two separate bowls of salted water. Drain the cubes thoroughly and cook for 3 minutes in a saucepan of boiling salted water (1½ tablespoons salt for 1 quart water). Plunge them into cold water and drain immediately. Cook the strips of eggplant skin in the same manner.

Combine the cubes and skins, and reheat them in a saucepan with the butter. Add the lemon zest and season with salt and pepper.

Before serving, reheat the fried eggplant for 4 minutes in a nonstick skillet with the cumin.

Presentation

Place the veal slices on the serving plates, arrange the fried eggplant slices on an angle with the veal slices. Line up the eggplant cubes and skin in a neat row next to the veal.

CHEF'S NOTE

Select a good quality of veal (preferably milk-fed). In France, our Limousin breed is excellent. The resting time (on a rack in the warm oven) is important; it allows the veal to relax and to take on a uniform pink color.

Sautéed veal kidneys

with absinthe, fresh almonds, and spiced white beans with tomato

FOR 4 SERVINGS

— FOR THE WHITE BEANS: 3 TOMATOES, 3 GARLIC CLOVES, 2 NEW ONIONS, 1 TABLE-SPOON OLIVE OIL, 1 BOUQUET GARNI (COMPOSED OF 1 SPRIG THYME, 1 BAY LEAF, AND A FEW SPRIGS PARSLEY), 1 PINCH GROUND CUMIN, 7 OUNCES SHELLED FRESH WHITE BEANS, 1 PINCH GROUND CURRY, 1 PINCH SAFFRON THREADS

— FOR THE VEAL KIDNEYS: 2 VEAL KIDNEYS (AS PALE AS POSSIBLE AND TRIMMED OF THEIR FAT), SALT, PEPPER, 2 TABLESPOONS OLIVE OIL

— FOR THE HERB SAUCE: ¼ CUP MARC DE PROVENCE*, ¼ CUP NOILLY PRAT OR OTHER DRY WHITE VERMOUTH, 1 PINCH POWDERED POULTRY BOUILLON, 1 PINCH GROUND ALLSPICE, 1 PINCH PAPRIKA, 2 TEASPOONS UNSALTED BUTTER, 1 TABLESPOON OLIVE OIL, 10 ABSINTHE LEAVES**, 8 SORREL LEAVES

— FOR THE PRESENTATION: A FEW FRESH ABSINTHE LEAVES**, A FEW SORREL LEAVES, 1 OUNCE SHELLED FRESH ALMONDS

The White Beans

Plunge the tomatoes into a saucepan of boiling water for 2 minutes. Drain, peel, and quarter the tomatoes, removing the pulp and seeds, collecting the juices in a bowl. Dice the flesh. Strain the juice to remove the seeds.

Peel and crush the garlic cloves. Peel and chop the onions and brown them in a saucepan with the olive oil. Add the juice from the tomatoes, bouquet garni, the garlic, cumin, and white beans. Add water to fill the saucepan about halfway, bring to a boil, and cook for 30 minutes over low heat. At the end of the cooking, add the diced tomato, curry powder, and saffron.

The veal kidneys

Preheat the oven to 350°F. Season the veal kidneys with salt and pepper. Heat the oil in a cast-iron skillet, and sear the kidneys over high heat, rounded-side down. Turn the kidneys and finish the cooking in the preheated oven for 5 to 6 minutes. Remove the kidneys from the oven, transfer to a rack and cover with aluminum foil. Let rest in the warm oven (turned off). (Place a tray under the rack to allow juices to run off.)

The herb sauce

Discard any excess fat from the skillet, deglaze with the marc de Provence, add the Noilly Prat and ½ cup water. Add the poultry bouillon, allspice and paprika. Bring to a boil, remove from the heat, and whisk the sauce, incorporating the butter and olive oil. Just before serving, chop the absinthe and the sorrel and add to the sauce.

Presentation

Place a little of the white beans on the edge of each plate, then add the kidneys. Spoon the herb sauce over and decorate with fresh absinthe and sorrel leaves. Sprinkle with fresh almonds.

* MARC DE PROVENCE *is white or clear brandy from Provence. Subtitute any good quality brandy, preferably clear.*

** IF ABSINTHE LEAVES *are not available, substitute a few drops of one of the newly marketed liqueurs created to imitate the flavor of the notorious absinthe alcohol, banned in the 1900s. A few drops of another popular French aperitif called Suze can also be substituted.*

CHEF'S NOTE

Poach the pears a day in advance; they will absorb the flavors of the spices better. This dessert can be enriched with a scoop of vanilla or pineapple ice cream.

For Health and Pleasure

« It flows from the hemispheres of a star, a universe of gold, a yellow cup full of miracles, the tiny fire of a vast planet ... »

Pablo Neruda
about the lemon.

GOLDEN FRUIT

THE LEMONS OF MENTON

Above:
A lemon seller with her
harvest of the famous
lemons of Menton.

ACCORDING TO LEGEND, MENTON'S FIRST TOURISTS were Adam and Eve. After much wandering, the unhappy couple found a place reminiscent of Paradise at Garavan Bay, just west of today's French-Italian border. Eve, a prudent traveler, would have taken from Eden a few lemons, for the road. On this new site, the divine citrus seeds grew well and so did, much later, the city of Menton. Lemons are often linked to Eden and eternal spring because the tree produces flowers and fruit year-round, intermingling its immaculate, satin-textured, fragrant, pale blossoms and its luminous golden orbs, both beautifully set off by a mass of broadleaved evergreen foliage. The mountains at Menton rise immediately behind the city, protecting trees from winter frosts. In this microclimate, much milder than that of northern Italy, citrus ripens as happily as in Sardinia. Commercial cultivation of lemons began here already in the fifteenth century and peaked between 1740 and 1840. At that time, most were grown in small gardens where the production per acre sometimes reached as high as 15,000 a year. After 1850, however, the breaking up of land holdings, the neglect of country lanes and paths, and the lack of a port that could handle steamships all contributed to the decline of this picturesque cottage industry. Then came the devastating, long-lasting freeze of 1956, followed soon after by a fungus called "mal sec" (Phoma tracheïphila Petri). The number of lemon trees in Menton dropped from 50,000 to 5,000. In 1964, yet another predator arrived, a variety of cochineal that still threatens many attempts to re-establish orchards today.

Despite of all these handicaps, lemon growing has come back to Menton. Instrumental has been the celebrated Lemon Festival or *Fête du Citron* which takes place here every year in February. Established in 1895 by four enterprising hotel owners, it has become the second biggest public festival of the French Riviera, after the Carnival of Nice. More than 200,000 people buy tickets for the lemon festival every year. The main attraction is the fantastic display of giant sculptures

made from lemons, organized into fifteen tableaux, spread out through the Biovès park. Stunning floats decorated with lemons move through the center city to the beach on weekends, while musicians and folk dancers liven up the public squares. On the day of Mardi Gras itself, a remarkable fireworks show rises over the water as the climax of the great moonlight parade.

Some renewal of lemon growing was required, if only to supply enough lemons for this festivity, and soon the local industry gathered momentum. The municipality, the Chamber of Agriculture, the Credit Agricole bank, and the growers themselves have been working hard to obtain a government label of origin for the Menton lemon. Terraced sites on mountainsides, are now enhanced with citrus orchards. Sometimes the lemons sold in local markets come from the private estates whose lovely walled gardens from the Belle Epoque and the 1920s have earned Menton the nickname "Garden City." The town itself owns the remarkable Carnolès Palace, once a princely residence, later a casino, and now an art museum. Situated right in the city center, its park boasts 137 varieties of citrus, a "National Collection," awarded this label formally by the National Scientific Institute (*Conservatoire des collections végétales spécialisées* or CCVS). Among its treasures are curiosities such as *Combava citrius hystrix*, the mandarin-variety Cléopatra and the Corsican citron. Still other varieties are grown only a few miles away in the Hanbury Botanical Gardens, just over the border in La Mortola, Italy.

Some new producers are experimenting with organic methods for fighting pests and planting old, resistant varieties like Eurêka or Le

Above:
A National Collection of citrus at the Carnolès Park in Menton.

Right:
From flower and fruit come essences and aromatic waters.

Mentonnais. At the same time, the National Agronomy Institute (INRA) is developing new ones that can thrive without spraying, like the Citron de Menton, which cooks appreciate for its rich essential oils, its slightly acidic flavor, and its heady aroma. Tests carried out in Corsica and Nice have confirmed that this variety really does give best results when grown in or around the city of Menton. In the gardens of the Bastide Saint Antoine, Jacques Chibois likes to experiment with citrus varieties, as lemon juice is rarely missing from his dishes.

Lemon growing in Menton has always combined health and pleasure, first of all in the fruit itself, so rich in vitamin C that sailors used it on sea voyages to prevent scurvy. There are also local medicinal products made from citrus—orange flower water and its essence (called *neroli* locally), or the health-giving syrup called "bitter water" (*aiga afra*), a very old traditional remedy. The lemon tree offers beauty, health, and enjoyment, and has earned its place in paradise.

Tuna marinated in lemon
and ginger with creamy fresh cheese

For 4 servings:

— For the tuna: 1⅓ pounds red tuna fillets, ½ teaspoon ground ginger, 1 tablespoon chopped black olives, 1 tablespoon finely chopped zest of untreated lemon, salt, pepper, ⅓ cup plus 4 teaspoons olive oil, juice of ½ lemon

— For the cucumber sauce: 1 cucumber, 1 teaspoon marc de Provence*, 1 tablespoon olive oil, salt, pepper

— For the fresh cheese: 1¼ ounces firm fresh *brousse***, 1 pinch zest of an untreated lemon, a few drops lemon juice, salt, pepper, ⅔ cup whipping cream

— For the presentation: 3 ounces purslane***, 12 basil leaves, 4 pinches white flower petals (roses, almond blossoms, etc.), 1 tablespoon julienne of untreated lemon zest, 1 teaspoon nigella seeds****, ½ teaspoon paprika flakes, salt, pepper

The tuna

Cut the tuna in ½-inch cubes and place in a bowl. Add the ginger, olives, and lemon zest. Season with salt and pepper. Just before serving, drizzle with the olive oil and lemon juice and toss gently.

The cucumber sauce

Peel the cucumber, slice into rounds and cook for 8 minutes in a saucepan of boiling salted water (1½ tablespoons salt for 1 quart water). Plunge the cucumber slices into cold water and drain immediately. Process to a purée with the marc de Provence, olive oil, salt, and pepper. Strain the purée through a fine sieve, pressing with the back of a spoon to squeeze out as much juice as possible.

The fresh cheese

Thoroughly mix the brousse, lemon zest and lemon juice together. Season with salt and pepper. Whip the cream to soft peaks and fold delicately into the brousse mixture. Chill in the refrigerator for 30 minutes.

Presentation

Rinse and dry the purslane. Chop the basil leaves finely. Pour a little of the cucumber sauce in the center of each plate. Spoon the seasoned tuna in a 2-inch band through the center of each plate. Using a soup spoon, form the cheese mixture into neat *quenelle* or oval shapes and place on top of the tuna. Sprinkle the purslane leaves and the flower petals harmoniously around each serving and top with the basil, lemon zest, nigella seeds, and paprika flakes.

* MARC DE PROVENCE *is white brandy from Provence. Subtitute any good quality brandy, preferably clear.*

** BROUSSE *is a creamy, white fresh cheese made from ewe's milk. Ricotta cheese is a good alternative.*

*** PURSLANE, *called* pourpier *in French, is a salad green or pot herb with thick, fleshy leaves. If not available, substitute other greens such as lamb's lettuce.*

**** NIGELLA *seeds are also called black onion seeds.*

CHEF'S NOTE

Buy a piece tuna cut from the center, avoiding, whenever possible, the tail. To prevent it from loosing its texture, season the tuna at the last moment, just before serving, because the lemon "cooks" the fish.

The Chef's Advice

COOKING WITH LEMON

Lemon juice is essential in Mediterranean cooking. I put lemon, the juice and/or the zest, in nearly all of my dishes. In the South, fruits and vegetables have a lot of flavor, thanks to the sun that helps them develop juices full of sweet and intense flavors. On the other hand, our fruits often lack a point of acidity.

Lemon is also good for the digestion. People often tell me: "Your food is very light, it leaves a freshness on the palate." The consumption of lemon provokes a maleic reaction in the stomach, immediately increasing the citric acid produced naturally by our systems during digestion (citric acid is instrumental in setting off fermentation).

In addition, flavors explode when lemon zest is added to a fruit salad or to strawberries. Be sure to choose only lemons that have not undergone chemical treatment. France's Alpes-Maritime region is lucky to have a lemon that merits the prestigious AOC (appellation d'origine contrôlée) classification, the Menton lemon. And, a lot of people here in the South of France have old lemon trees in their gardens, such as those here at our Bastide. If you are not lucky enough to grow your own garden lemons, buy organic lemons. Almost all other lemons are treated after being picking to prevent them from spoiling. What's more, to make them prettier, they are waxed. This type of lemon is to be avoided if you don't want to ruin your recipes.

ESCOFFIER
AND THE PRODUCE OF PROVENCE

T HE ENGLISH GASTRONOME Elizabeth David once pondered the ways in which rustic peasant dishes might enter the higher spheres of culinary art. She pictured star chef Auguste Escoffier transforming the rough country fare of his childhood, adapting his mother's "dish of sliced potatoes and artichoke hearts baked with olive oil and garlic and scented with wild thyme," to the tastes of his elegant urban clientele. She imagined him replacing the olive oil with butter and meat essence, and thyme and garlic with fashionable truffles (also a peasant ingredient, unbeknownst to his public, David points out). Escoffier's mother might make a meal of such a preparation, adding a handful of olives and a few figs for dessert. But in London and Paris, it would become merely the vegetable accompanying *Carré d'agneau Mistral*. David's fantasy illustrates how chefs like Escoffier often got their inspiration. For example, the dish of *artichokes à la barigoule*, an Escoffier favorite, began as peasant food, then became middle class, then gastronomic. The country version was simply small, very young artichokes grilled or stewed whole with other vegetables (according to René Jouveau, in *La Cuisine provençale de tradition populaire*). By 1900, the recipe published in a famous cookbook by Reboul (*La Cuisinière provençale*) used large artichokes baked with a meat stuffing. Reboul's recipes were intended for the standardized middle-class family cooking called *cuisine bourgeoise*. His selection included many northern French dishes using, for example, béchamel sauce, which was rarely, if ever, found in southern peasant food. And finally Escoffier, in his *Culinary Art*, not only stuffs the artichokes but serves them braised in meat juice, much as in Elizabeth David's example. Today, everything has gone full circle. Young chefs in Provence are again prepare *artichokes à la barigoule* as a dish of fresh, very young, lightly stewed vegetables. No meat, no stuffing, natural juices instead of a sauce. The same cooks now love rustic ingredients such as olive oil, garlic, and wild thyme.

Escoffier himself, it must be said, defended regional produce at every opportunity, never spurning his simple Provençal origins. He began working in 1859 at the age of thirteen as an apprentice in his uncle's establishment in Nice. Fifty years later he celebrated his Jubilee as a famous chef. Along the way, this blacksmith's son had invented haute cuisine as we know it today, a world in which a cook could become a star. In his memoirs, he vehemently defends garlic, the "object of an inexplicable aversion." He insists that "it would be a mistake and a sacrilege to deprive ourselves of a condiment as necessary as garlic simply because it bears a name which outmoded prejudice has rendered suspect. If we could give it a new and pleasing name, the prettiest society women would be crazy about it" (Auguste Escoffier, *Memories of My Life*, translation Laurence Escoffier, Van Nostrand Reinhold, 1997).

The great man's imagination was as lively in business as behind a stove, especially when he was seeking out the best and freshest ingredients. His most famous creation was the peach Melba, made with fresh, dead-ripe peaches and named for a famous singer. Following on the success of this dessert, Escoffier began taking an interest in the market gardeners of Montreuil near Paris, who grew peaches against south-facing walls. From there, he moved on to the growers of the Rhône valley (who continue to produce wonderful peaches today). He negotiated contracts with them to purchase and preserve their best and most flavorful fruit. In 1911, some 15,000 pieces of fruit were processed. In 1914, this figure was already

Opposite:
Escoffier was born
in the house that
today has become
his museum.

approaching 100,000 when World War I put an end to the project.

Asparagus growing also captured Escoffier's attention. The chef noticed that the old baron de Rothschild, when he dined at Monte-Carlo, preferred green asparagus, as did the English habitués of the Savoy in London. Escoffier alone ordered so much green asparagus to satisfy his public that he sent prices sky high. He then went to the little town of Lauris (near Lourmarin, in the heart of Provence's asparagus country), and proposed to the local farmers that they grow green as well as white varieties. The older ones adamantly refused to change their methods, but one young man agreed to take the risk. His success far outstripped all predictions.

Escoffier's greatest adventure along these lines was with tomatoes. In 1892, he relates in his *Memories*, tomatoes were preserved only as purée in thick glass bottles like those used for champagne. It took the chef fifteen years of research to organize the production of 2,000 cans of whole crushed tomatoes which he had delivered directly to the Savoy. He was soon imitated in both Italy and then America, where the practice became general. Escoffier also set up industrial processing of pickles until 1914, based on a recipe of his own invention.

His experiments stopped only with his death. Until the end he remained convinced that "French soil has good fortune to produce naturally and in abundance the best vegetables, fruit and wines in the world." Today's young chefs are more open to the cuisines of other cultures and climates, but like Escoffier, they remain close to whatever region nourished them from the start.

Purple, green, and wild asparagus
with tarragon and balsamic vinaigrette

FOR 4 SERVINGS:
— FOR THE ASPARAGUS: 6 GREEN ASPARAGUS, 7 PURPLE PROVENÇAL ASPARAGUS, 6 WILD ASPARAGUS, 3½ TABLESPOONS UNSALTED BUTTER, ½ TABLESPOON MINCED FRESH TARRAGON, PEPPER, 1 TEASPOON CRÈME FRAÎCHE, A FEW DROPS LEMON JUICE, SALT
— FOR THE *COULIS* OR SAUCE: ½ RED BELL PEPPER, ½ YELLOW BELL PEPPER, SALT
— FOR THE PRESENTATION: 1½ TABLESPOONS OLIVE OIL, SCANT ¼ CUP BALSAMIC VINEGAR

The asparagus

Peel any tough ends from the green and purple asparagus using a vegetable peeler, tie them in bundles and cook for 4 to 5 minutes, depending upon their size and quality, in a large pan of boiling salted water (1½ tablespoons salt for 1 quart water). Test for doneness by inserting the tip of a knife into the stem ends. Cook the tiny wild asparagus in the same manner for 2 to 3 minutes until tender.

Rinse the asparagus under cold water and drain. Place them in a skillet with the butter, tarragon, a scant ⅔ cup water, and a pinch of pepper. Bring to a boil, add the crème fraîche, and let reduce for 5 minutes. Just before serving, roll the asparagus in the skillet to coat them well with the cooking juices and add the lemon juice.

The coulis

Core and seed the bell peppers, cut into slices. Cook for 5 minutes in a saucepan filled with boiling salted water (1½ tablespoons salt for 1 quart water). Drain and rinse the peppers under cold water. Thoroughly process the red and yellow peppers separately, then strain separately through a fine sieve to obtain two very fine purées.

The presentation

Divide the asparagus among the warm serving plates. Drizzle each serving with a little olive oil. Add a point of the red and yellow pepper *coulis* to each plate, and finish with a few drops of balsamic vinegar. Serve warm.

CHEF'S NOTE

It is important to cook the asparagus in a large quantity of boiling water. Before that, gather the asparagus in bunches and tie with kitchen string. The ends should be trimmed to the same length. Save the trimmed ends for another preparation such as in a sauce or a soup.

Pageot with fennel,
Lemon, and sautéed apricots

For 4 servings:
— For the vegetables: 2 fennel bulbs, 5 apricots, 2 tablespoons olive oil, salt, pepper, 2 teaspoons unsalted butter
— For the sauce: 4¼ ounces new onions, 1 clove garlic, 2 tablespoons olive oil, 3 sprigs dried fennel, 1 pinch powdered poultry bouillon
— For the pageot*: 4 fillets pageot, salt, pepper, 1 tablespoon olive oil, 2 teaspoons unsalted butter, a few drops lemon juice
— For the presentation: a handful of young beet leaves, a few petals of untreated roses, 4 fresh fennel flowers (or other aromatic herb such as lemon verbena or rosemary)

The vegetables

Rinse the fennel bulbs and cut them horizontally into ¼-inch thick slices, removing the heart and any woody parts. Cook it in a large pan of boiling salted water (1½ tablespoons salt to 1 quart water), then plunge into cold water and drain immediately.

Cut the apricots in half, remove the pits, then slice them into uniform wedges. Sauté the apricots in a skillet with 1 tablespoon very hot olive oil, turning to brown quickly on both sides. Season with salt and pepper; add the butter, the remaining olive oil, and the fennel.

The sauce

Peel and chop the onions. Peel and crush the garlic cloves. Heat the olive oil in a saucepan over low heat. Add the onions, garlic clove, and dried fennel sprigs. Cook for 1 minute without browning, then add 1 cup water and the poultry bouillon powder. Cover and cook for 10 minutes. Pour this liquid over the apricot-fennel mixture, bring to a boil and cook for 1 minute.

The pageot

Preheat the oven to 400°F. Season the pageot fillets with salt and pepper. Warm the oil and butter together in a non-stick skillet and sauté the fish for 2 to 3 minutes on each side. Transfer to a non-stick baking sheet and finish cooking in the oven for 4 to 5 minutes. Sprinkle each fillet with the lemon juice after the cooking.

Presentation

Rinse and dry the beet leaves. Arrange them on the serving plates. Top with a little of the fennel and apricot mixture, then with a pageot fillet. Bring the sauce to a boil and add the rose petals, finely chopped. Spoon the sauce over the fish and stud with the fennel flowers.

* PAGEOT *is a marine fish found in the Mediterranean that is similar to a sea bream. If it is not available, use sea bream or porgy.*

CHEF'S NOTE

Select apricots that are ripe but firm, so that they remain presentable after cooking. If you don't have untreated rose petals, use the leaves of small endive.

The Chef's Advice

SWEET-ACID AND SWEET-SOUR

In Provençal cooking, we use a lot of lemon, and this is often to bring out the sweetness of fruits or vegetables that ripen in the sun of the South and are therefore particularly rich in natural sugars. The acid-sweet combination is not the same as the sweet-and-sour so much appreciated in the cuisines of the North and East, as well as in the United States. It's important to know that classic "sweet-sour" is based on vinegar or acetic acid, while lemons contain citric acid.

Lemon juice comes directly from the fruit, while vinegar, whether based on apples, grapes or other fruits, has been transformed through the introduction of yeasts or enzymes. Vinegar has been fermented, an extra step away from the fresh fruit, which makes its essences much more volatile.

Put a drop of lemon juice on a strawberry and you will intensify the taste, because all fruits already contain some citric acid. In other words, citric acid reinforces flavors without overwhelming them. If you try the same experiment with vinegar, you'll find that the taste of the strawberry is masked by the acidity of the vinegar, which is much more violent and prickles the nose.

Finally, don't forget balsamic vinegar, which has become very popular in recent years. This popularity comes from the fact that the alcohol this vinegar contains evaporates quickly when it is added to a preparation and the remaining thick vinegar evolves toward sugar. This vinegar in a nectar with a sweet and aromatic flavor, less powerful and less aggressive than other vinegars.

A SMALL FAMILY FARM

LES OLIVADES

Polyculture of such quality requires personal attention on the part of the growers.

O N THEIR FAMILY FARM in a western suburb of the city of Toulon, Daniel and Denise Vuillon specialize in vegetables selected for flavor. They well remember the day in 1991 when the manager of the neighboring supermarket explained to them that taste was only number seven on the criteria used by their purchasing department! The store also wanted vegetables of uniform size and appearance and, therefore, refused to buy produce grown in the open air. Daniel, a third-generation market farmer, decided then and there to promote different aims and values. Today at Les Olivades, his family grows high-quality vegetables while experimenting with parallel distribution methods. Their clientele includes several famous chefs from as far away as Paris and Geneva.

The Vuillons cultivate many heirloom varieties, but preservation of the past is not their first concern. Fine flavor remains their main standard, whether the variety is old or new, local, or from foreign parts. All vegetables, of course, vary in taste according to the soil in which they are grown. Among the tomato cultivars that do well at Les Olivades are the Andine cornue, Brandywine (America's favorite!), and Evergreen. Other exotics such as Black Russian and Rose de Berne often win taste tests organized during their July Tomato Festival. The Vuillons are not collectors but they do grow more than 110 different tomato varieties. They work closely with the Kokopelli Association, which helps preserve endangered varieties worldwide, collaborating closely with the Seed Savers Exchange in the United States. The founder of this association, Dominique Guillet, preserves heirloom vegetables not recognized on the official listings, often in opposition to restrictive European regulations. He urges the free sale of "Seeds Without Boundaries" and participates in international movements to defend biodiversity. He resists the influence of multinationals, who would impose infertile hybrid seed and limit consumer choices to their own patented varieties, many of which have been genetically modified.

The Olivades farm is threatened today by controversial urban expansion projects.

The farm Les Olivades has been in Daniel's family for more than a century. The house is an old *bastide* surrounded by ten acres of open-field vegetables and three acres of greenhouses. The alkaline clay earth is sometimes difficult to plough, but gives a far more pungent taste to the crops than sandy soils. Luckily, the fields are protected from the fierce north wind by a convenient hill, and most are set on a gentle rise sloping southeast. Thanks to the Canal de Provence, they are naturally irrigated by water from the Verdon river. The drip system linking the canal to the plants is never used to convey fertilizers or pesticides. Nonetheless, high-quality crops are produced thanks to the care the family gives to its soil and to seed selection.

None of this is easy. In recent years, all the neighboring farms have disappeared—some because of the new fast train line, others because of high- tension electricity wires, still others when shopping centers filled up this zone on the edge of the city of Toulon. Nine acres of the Vuillons' land have already been expropriated by the municipality. Today, a battle rages around a project for a new tram line, which could easily pass elsewhere. Denise is amazed. Toulon has gone to the trouble of setting up a permanent Educational Farm Project to show schoolchildren how farmers used to live. Why would their city not be proud of this precious and authentic farm, still very much alive and operating, which bears witness to the greenbelt that used to be?

But nostalgia is not the main point. The Vuillons are building for the future. Their daughter, Edithe Bramerie, worked for years in

Right:
The Vuillons also
grow many herbs and
aromatics such as these
multicolored basils.

Manhattan as an architect. She became familiar with the Community Supported Agriculture program, which links small producers and consumers directly, creating new and safer markets for the former, while providing much better-quality produce to the latter. This allowed small market gardens to defend their very existence close to major cities. The system set up in France involves the selling of shares in the year's crops. Each shareholder receives a weekly basket of the best fresh produce, with any excess given to charity. This particular alternative distribution network in France is called the *Association pour le maintien d'une agriculture paysanne* (AMAP). Thanks in part to the Vuillons, an organization that first developed in Provence has now spread to other regions. The Olivades farm offers a fine example of home-grown globalization, deeply rooted in local soil but constructively linked to far-away places in a shared defense of variety rather than uniformity, proximity rather than expansion.

The choice for diversity sometimes has surprising results. Among the crops grown at Les Olivades are the bamboo-like reeds (*Arondo donax*) used everywhere in the region as windbreaks. But for some reason, this part of the coastline produces a quality which can be used in making reeds for fine musical instruments like saxophones, oboes, and clarinets! This is yet another example of what Daniel calls "the soil's signature." The Vuillons have proven that genuine progress can be made today, with a little effort and care, in a manner that respects quality and flavor while remaining profitable for small producers.

Minestrone of fresh fruits
and vegetables, with frosty olive oil

For 4 servings:
— For the minestrone: ½ medium (2 ounces) zucchini, ¼ bulb (2 ounces) fennel, 1 small (2 ounces) carrot, 3 vanilla beans, 1 quart (4 cups) mineral water, 6½ tablespoons granulated sugar, 8 leaves basil, 6½ ounces (¼ cup diced) strawberries, ½ peeled mango, 1 peeled kiwi, zest and juice of 1 untreated lime.
— For the frosty olive oil: ½ cup mild olive oil, ½ tablespoon granulated sugar
— For the presentation: a few wild strawberries

The minestrone

Rinse the zucchini and fennel, peel and rinse the carrot, and cut all of the vegetables into ¼-inch cubes. In a large saucepan of lightly salted boiling water (2 teaspoons salt to 1 quart water) cook the vegetables separately for 1 to 3 minutes, one after the other, in the following order: zucchini, fennel, and carrot. They should remain slightly crunchy. Rinse in cold water, drain, then combine the three vegetables.

Split the vanilla beans in half lengthwise with a paring knife. Place in a saucepan with the mineral water and sugar. Bring to a boil and simmer over low heat for 5 minutes. Scrape the seeds from the vanilla beans with the tip of a paring knife, return the seeds to the liquid without the pods. (Reserve the pods for the decoration.) Chop the basil leaves finely, add to the liquid along with the vegetables and let infuse, refrigerated, for 1 to 2 hours. Dice the strawberries, mango, and kiwi into ¼-inch cubes and add to the vegetables. Grate the lime zest and add to the mixture along with the lime juice. Return to the refrigerator.

The frosty olive oil

Thoroughly process or blend the olive oil with the sugar and ½ tablespoon water. Pour into a fancy ice cube tray, filling each cubicle with about ¼-inch of the mixture. Place in the freezer to harden.

Presentation

Pour the minestrone into chilled, shallow serving bowls. Add one or more cubes of the frosty olive oil. Garnish with wild strawberries.

CHEF'S NOTE

Don't forget to put the bowls in the freezer several hours before serving the minestrone.

OLIVE OIL

A MOUNTAIN MILL

THE HILL TOWN OF SPÉRACÈDES clings to a cliff west of Grasse. The Baussy family owns two olive-oil mills here: the "old" one, used for centuries by the lords of the castle, no longer functions, and the "new" one below has just celebrated its hundredth birthday. Recently renovated, it uses the latest technology. No more millstones, no more pressing mats piled up to filter the oil, no more press at all, but a series of stainless-steel mixers which produce oil quickly by centrifugal pressure according to the new European standards. The Baussy name has been established in the region since the thirteenth century, linked to generations of millers. But now the family is thinking of the future.

Jacques Chibois, one of their clients, explains that "thanks to this new technology, the olives don't suffer. Everything happens fast. Before, to crush them, people added water to get a kind of thick olive paste that went through the press. During this time the olives were in contact with the air and might oxidize. And you were lucky if you had a miller who worried about hygiene! If he did not clean his equipment after each pressing and the customer before you had rotting olives, your oil would be spoiled." Today at Spéracèdes, any private person with a crop of at least 80 kilos of olives can bring them to the mill, by appointment. The oil will be ready just two hours later with no risk of contamination since separate mixers allow treatment of several lots at the same time without intermingling. The mill operates from November through April. Half of the olives treated come from the department of the Alpes-Maritimes, which has good soil and trees untouched by frost for centuries. But this region, to the east, is both overbuilt and mountainous—factors which inhibit expansion of existing orchards. The other half of the olives pressed comes from the Var department to the west. Here the soil is actually better for vineyards but there are large flat areas available for new plantations. One customer in the Var just set out 8,000 olive trees with the help of

subsidies from the European Union. Everywhere owners are modernizing, paying more attention to upkeep of their trees, and installing drip irrigation.

Modern transportation in refrigerated trucks allows the Baussy to mix different varieties of olives picked in various places, wherever they grow best, without sacrificing the qualities that justify their prestigious "AOC" (or controlled origin) label. They like best the Cailletier olive of the Alpes Maritimes which comes from a tall, slender tree and is harvested on nets spread out on the ground. This is a mild, fragrant olive which the Baussys buy from growers at altitudes where it is not necessary to spray against the Mediterranean fruit fly. To add a bit of zip, they combine it with more ardent varieties such as the Picholine from Les Baux and the fat Anglandau from Haute Provence.

The actual pressing of olives can cause pollution. Olives are 50% water, and more was added in the past. For the last twenty years, millers paid a special anti-pollution tax. Today this liquid, waste for the mill but of natural origin, can be recycled as a fertilizer. Better still, the laboratories of one of the Grasse perfume manufacturers (a Baussy sister works there) have successfully transformed this waste into an anti-oxidizing agent that can be used in the food industry.

The Baussy family is deeply rooted in the business

of olives. One of the sons says, "Just a whiff of that smell from the mill and you are hooked forever!" Another brother specializes in food salons and fairs. He has constructed a small model mill so that, using olives that have been frozen for transportation, he can show tourists in other regions how oil is produced by his family at home. Those who stay in Spéracèdes often show the mill to groups of school children. They are transforming the old village mill into a museum of country life (*écomusée*).

Jacques Chibois shares the Baussy's passion. Several hundred ancient trees grow on his terraces of the Bastide Saint-Antoine, among them many of the Cailletier variety. When the chef first had the trees pruned in 1998 after years of neglect, visitors said to him, "Monsieur Chibois, you are murdering nature!" But those who know farming know that fruit trees need pruning to prosper. Both health and production increased enormously after this task was completed. At the Bastide, some olives are picked and pressed green, another batch just as they begin to turn brown, a third lot when they are half black, and the last ones dead ripe, black and oily. With these products, the cook can create blends of oils adapted for different uses: One pressing tastes more like artichokes, another more like almonds.

Above:
The painter Renoir admired this foliage, "sad in grey weather, resonant in the sun and silvery in the wind."

Right:
The mysteries of fruit transformed into oil

The pleasure provided by olive oil comes second only to its health-giving qualities, so celebrated today that it is hard to recall a time when northerners regarded this wonderful tree with contempt. The French novelist Stendhal wrote that "no tree in the world could be uglier; they always look doddery and stunted." In 1861 the English poet Swinburne, noted for excesses of every kind, called olive trees "blank, beastly and senseless . . . like a mad cabbage gone indigestible." Perhaps if he had regularly consumed their oil, he would have been in a better mood? Today this majestic tree, much admired, symbolizes the essence of Mediterranean lifestyles. And since only 5% of the olive oil consumed in France is produced on its own territory, this cottage industry's expansion seems destined to succeed.

Provençal artichokes
with cèpe mushrooms and parmesan shavings

FOR 4 SERVINGS:
— FOR THE VEGETABLES: 1 POUND FRESH CÈPE MUSHROOMS, 1½ TABLESPOONS UNSALTED BUTTER, 3 TABLESPOONS OLIVE OIL, SALT, 8 SMALL PURPLE ARTICHOKES*, ½ LEMON, PEPPER, 1 CLOVE GARLIC, ¼ CUP POULTRY BOUILLON, 1 TABLESPOON CREAM, 1 TABLESPOON DRY WHITE WINE, 3 SPRIGS FLAT-LEAF PARSLEY.
— FOR THE PRESENTATION: 2 OUNCES PARMESAN CHEESE

The vegetables

Scrape clean the stem ends of the cèpes to remove any dirt, rinse quickly under cold water, pat dry. Cut the cèpes into ¼-inch slices and sauté them in a nonstick skillet with the butter, 1 tablespoon olive oil, and a little salt. When the cèpes are well browned, transfer to a plate and set aside in a warm oven (turned off). Remove the leaves from the artichokes, keeping the bottom, heart, and 2 inches of the stem; rub immediately with the lemon half. Place the artichokes in a pan with a little water, salt, pepper, and a tablespoon of the olive oil. Cover and cook for 5 minutes. Peel and crush the garlic clove. Drain the artichokes and sauté them with the remaining tablespoon olive and the garlic. Combine the cèpes with the artichokes in a sauté pan. Add the poultry bouillon, bring to a boil, and cook for 2 minutes. Add the cream and the white wine. Correct the seasoning if necessary. Mince the parsley and sprinkle over the vegetables.

Presentation

Arrange the artichokes in shallow serving dishes, fan the cèpes out around the artichokes, and spoon the cooking liquid around. With a vegetable peeler, shave long, thin curls of the Parmesan and sprinkle over each serving.

* THE ARTICHOKES used here are the tender violet de Provence artichokes, also called poivrade. Different from the globe-shaped artichokes of Brittany, this smaller, cone-shaped variety is tinged with purple tips. These are not available in the U.S., but 8 small "globe" artichokes that weigh about 6 ounces each are a good substitute.

CHEF'S NOTE

Salt the cèpes little by little, tasting frequently. To help them brown nicely, don't hesitate to add a little more olive oil. They can be drained at the end of the cooking before preparing the sauce.

Pan-seared john dory
with anise-flavored celery and artichokes

FOR 4 SERVINGS :
— FOR THE VEGETABLES: 12 PURPLE ARTICHOKES*, ½ LEMON, 1 ONION, 1 CLOVE
GARLIC, 1 RIB CELERY, 1 TABLESPOON OLIVE OIL, ¼ CUP DRY WHITE WINE, A FEW
DROPS PASTIS**, JUICE OF 1 LEMON, SALT, PEPPER
— FOR THE SAUCE: 6 CELERY LEAVES, 1 TABLESPOON ZEST OF AN UNTREATED LEMON,
2 TABLESPOONS OLIVE OIL, 1 TABLESPOON UNSALTED BUTTER, SALT, PEPPER, A FEW
DROPS LEMON JUICE
— FOR THE JOHN DORY: 4 LARGE FILLETS OF JOHN DORY*** WITHOUT THE SKIN,
SALT, PEPPER, 1 TABLESPOON OLIVE OIL, 1 TABLESPOON UNSALTED BUTTER, A FEW
DROPS LEMON JUICE
— FOR THE PRESENTATION: 4 CELERY LEAVES, 12 BLACK NIÇOISE OLIVES

The vegetables

Remove leaves from the artichokes, keeping the bottom, heart and
about 2 inches of the stem, rubbing each immediately with the lemon
half. Peel and chop the onion. Peel and crush the garlic. Chop the celery.
Heat the oil in a sauté pan, sweat the onion and garlic and sauté, then
add the artichokes. Add the celery, white wine, pastis, and lemon juice.
Season with salt and pepper, add ½ cup water and cook, covered, for
15 minutes over low heat. Let the artichokes cool in their cooking liquid.

The sauce

Remove the cooking liquid from the artichokes and process or blend
thoroughly with 6 celery leaves, the lemon zest, olive oil, butter, salt, and
pepper. Strain and press the sauce through a fine sieve. Pour into a
saucepan, bring to boil, and remove from the heat. Correct seasoning if
necessary, then add the lemon juice.

The John Dory

Season the fish fillets with salt and pepper. Heat the oil and butter gently in a non-stick skillet, add the fish fillets and gradually increase the temperature. Cook until firm to the touch, about 5 minutes, turning the fillets one or two times. Drizzle the fish with lemon juice at the end of the cooking.

Presentation

Spoon a little of the sauce on each serving plate. Place one whole artichoke on the edge of each plate with a John Dory fillet in the center. Cut the remaining artichokes into thin slices, and divide among the servings. Decorate with the black olives and tiny, tender celery leaves.

* THE ARTICHOKES *used here are the tender* violet de Provence *artichokes, also called* poivrade. *Different from the globe-shaped artichokes of Brittany, this smaller, cone-shaped variety is tinged with purple tips. These are not available in the U.S., but 8 small "globe" artichokes that weigh about 6 ounces each are a good substitute.*

** PASTIS *is a licorice/anise flavored aperitif particularly popular in Southern France.*

*** JOHN DORY, *common in the Mediterranean, can be difficult to find in the U.S. Snapper is a good alternative.*

CHEF'S NOTE

For the flavor balance of this recipe, choose perfect, pale green celery leaves—they will give the sauce a lovely flavor, milder than the strong taste of darker leaves. Be very careful when cooking the John Dory: begin cooking over low heat and increase the temperature gradually to avoid damaging the delicate flesh. In this way, it remains tender and flavorful.

The Chef's Advice

GARLIC OIL

I use garlic much more for its redolent aroma than for its taste: it's the scent of garlic that evokes the flavor, and not the contrary. If we eat raw garlic, we have at the same time the taste and the smell of garlic, but the scent persists well after the taste has disappeared, which can very unpleasant. What's more, once they are cut open, raw garlic and onion oxidize and become toxic after only ten minutes making digestion occasionally difficult. Using garlic oil is a way to avoid this.

To make garlic oil, choose an oil that is as neutral as possible, such as peanut oil. Mix the oil and raw garlic in a food processor or blender to make a paste. Warm the mixture over low heat for 15 to 20 minutes without allowing it to boil so that it simmers slowly without oxidizing. After the cooking, there will be no more fermentation, nor any oxidation and the aromas will have been captured by the oil. Next, the garlic and oil can be separated to be used separately. For example, the garlic oil can be added to a dish at the last moment. This will immediately impart the aroma of the garlic, and will scent the taste without causing any unpleasantness.

GRASSROOTS COOKING SCHOOLS
in Provence

GREAT COOKS TRANSFORM CHOICE RAW MATERIALS into works of art, and their vocation often begins at home. When Jacques Chibois was ten years old, his family moved to Limoges because his father, a miller, had developed an allergy to flour. To keep the family afloat, Madame Chibois opened a little bistro in town which met with great success. Jacques, as a boy, gave her a helping hand.

French family cuisine remains closely linked to local produce and regional character. In Provence, several grassroots associations have been busily working to preserve this heritage. They provide a link among generations and also between small, rural localities and the outside world. Some contribute to the survival of small farms by helping growers reach a wider public to market quality produce and crafts. This is always a sharing—never a staging—organized by a purely local population, but also open to outsiders.

In the Var department east of Marseille, *Les Amis de la Cuisine* have been organizing workshops for over twenty years. These take place two or three days a week in a house rented from the township of La Roquebrussane. Food lovers learn how to make traditional dishes like cod in red wine sauce, or parsnips au gratin (the parsnip was once known, if not common, in Provence). "We don't use the techniques of fancy cooking, but just homestyle," explains the president of the Association, Madame Caulet. "But you never know, someone might be inspired and go on to be a great chef!" she adds. Carefully selected volunteers do the teaching—they must know how to explain the dishes and their cultural heritage. Typical is Myriam Desestries, a specialist in herbs used for both cooking and healing. In spite of administrative hassles, the Association has so far resisted pressures to become either commercial or touristy. Its members want to keep the carefree atmosphere of good fun that has thus far meant so much to participants, including summer visitors from Japan and Germany.

Old copper pots, beautiful as they are, count less than the cook's experience. Culinary quarrels of yesteryear

M. THIERS ET LA BRANDADE DÉFENDUE

uls, sans témoins, les deux vieux amis, Thiers et Mignet, se régalaient de la fameuse brandade, sévèrement
ée par ordonnance des médecins. Mme Thiers, qui les croyait occupés à quelque travail important et sérieux,
n étonnée, quand un jour elle les prit en flagrant délit. — Voir l'anecdote et la recette dans ce numéro.

OMMAIRE DU NUMÉRO. — Notre Concours : distribution des prix (fin). — MENUS DU DIMANCHE. *Déjeuner* : crevettes sautées à la
nde; brandade de morue; escalopes de porc frais grillées; camembert à l'anglaise; figues sèches aux noix, accompagnées de grenades. *Dîner* :
ox-tail; barbue à la sauce ivoire; côtelettes de veau à la Talleyrand; albran rôti (petit canard sauvage); celeris-raves à la crème; gâteau Vert-
— Lunch d'Enfants : chocolat au lait; brioches; diablotins aux amandes; petits-fours navettes; boules de neige. — Recettes régionales:
à la royale, selon la mode du Périgord. — Apprêts de truffes (suite) : truffes au madère; truffes à l'italienne; truffes en bateaux. — Recettes
ères : crème d'avoine au bouillon (potage); bœuf bouilli en sauce piquante.

Polémique d'antan...

In the Vaucluse department, an association called Welcome to Peasant Provence (*Accueil en Provence paysanne*) aims at showing travelers how small-time farmers live and work today. Nineteen members work together through a Center for the Study of Agricultural Techniques. New participants must first review their heritage through winter workshops over a five-year period. Two of these (two weeks each) are about cooking. Above all, explains president Sylvette Mouries, "We want our members to welcome visitors to their farms in a sincere and friendly manner, while helping them learn about what we make and produce here." One result of these efforts has been a cookbook, *Recettes de Provence paysanne*, with a preface by Dr. Bernard Ély, a distinguished scholar of local traditions who, far ahead of the fashion, promoted Provençal cuisine for its wholesome and health-giving virtues.

Among the members of Welcome to Peasant Provence is Paula Chauvin of the Gerbaud Farm in Lourmarin. She had a city job when she inherited some sixty acres of wild hillside around an abandoned farmstead, where she now grows drought-resistant aromatics for medicinal purposes and culinary uses. She cooks up wonderful meals for groups of at least twelve people using recipes from the Association cookbook such as olive cake and tomato tart. Visitors first tour her fields of thyme, sage, lavender, and rosemary, learning the characteristics of each plant and its growing tips before tasting. Paula explains, "In the old days, people added herbs for health reasons. Today we have prescription drugs and we think mainly of taste. But herbs are good for both purposes." Her field-to-table approach has been very successful.

In the Bouches-du-Rhône department, an active Interdepartmental Conservancy for Mediterranean Cuisines is sponsored by the Chamber of Commerce of the city of Arles. On weekends, moving from village to village, it offers classes to hundreds of cooks who often attend together as families. The man who organizes these courses, Jean-Marc Biojoux, also travels abroad to advertise home fare—to Turkey, for example, to present Arlesian hazelnuts. An association further west called the Spice Trail, founded fifteen years ago in Montpellier by Philippe and Soraya Lagarrigue often joins forces with the Conservancy. They offer cooking classes inspired by more than 200 key ingredients. Their recipes like those of the other associations are easy to make. The idea, according to Madame Lagarrigue, is to both "learn about our traditions and have fun." Finally, the château de Rousty (situated between Saint-Rémy-de-Provence and Tarascon) has been chosen by these last two associations as the site of a new project: a School of Taste and of Olive Culture. The domain has many attractions, including an amazing olive-oil mill built in 1703, the largest in Europe at that time. The owners, a mother-and-daughter team, are descendants of the original sixteenth century château builders. Mademoiselle du Lac is restoring the old mill but also setting up a modern one nearby. Rousty's oil has famous Controlled Appellation label of the Baux Valley and its production is entirely organic. Mademoiselle du Lac explains with enthusiasm, "I want Rousty to become a pilot project for producers aiming to combine environmental awareness with fine flavor."

Each region, each association has its story, its style of management, its ways of reaching the public. But the organizers, varied as they are, have the same approach to the changes affecting country life today. This is neither nostalgia nor the cynical postcard marketing. These passionate defenders of home cooking are all working hard so that the past may feed the future in every way.

Above:
Today's chefs owe much to generations of inventive family cooks.

Right:
The mortar and pestle have their place, even today.

Rack of sucking pig

with winter vegetables and tonka bean sauce

For 4 servings:
— For the vegetables: 7 ounces (1 slice) winter squash*, 7 ounces (2 medium) carrots, 6½ ounces (3 small) turnips, 7 ounces (4 or 5) Jerusalem artichokes, 1½ tablespoons unsalted butter, salt, pepper, 1 pinch ground cinnamon, 1 pinch grated tonka bean**, 1 pinch grated nutmeg
— For the suckling pig: 1 rack of farm-raised suckling pig (prepared by the butcher with backbone removed, frenched, and tied), salt, pepper, 1 cup olive oil, 2 garlic cloves, 2 medium onions, 1 bunch aromatic herbs (bay leaf, marjoram or oregano, rosemary, savory, thyme), 2 tablespoons softened unsalted butter, 2 tablespoons honey
— For the jus: 1 pinch grated tonka bean, 1½ tablespoons unsalted butter, a few drops lemon juice
— For the presentation: 1 teaspoon sesame seeds, 1 teaspoon sunflower seeds

The vegetables

Peel and rinse the squash, carrots, turnips, and Jerusalem artichokes, and slice them into ⅛-inch thick rounds. Braise each vegetable separately, placing each in a sauté pan with a little of the butter, 2 tablespoons water, salt, and pepper.

Season the squash with cinnamon, the carrots with the grated tonka bean, and the turnips with nutmeg. Leave the Jerusalem artichokes plain.

On a buttered, oven-proof serving platter, arrange the vegetable slices around the edge, alternating by color: the squash, carrot, turnip, and Jerusalem artichokes. Before serving, drizzle the vegetables with 2 table-spoons water and reheat gently in the oven.

The suckling pig

Preheat the oven to 300°F. Season the prepared rack with salt and pepper and brown in the olive oil, in a shallow cast-iron roasting pan on the stove. Cut the onions and garlic in half (with their skins) and place around the meat, along with the aromatic herbs. Drizzle with ½ cup water, cover with aluminum foil, and bake for 2 hours.

Increase the oven temperature to 350°F. Melt the butter and honey together and brush over the meat. Return the meat to the oven to brown, uncovered, for 30 minutes. Transfer to a platter, and let rest in the warm oven (turned off).

The jus

Add 1 tablespoon water to the juices in the roasting pan and bring to a boil over high heat, stirring to loosen the flavorful browned bits that stick to the bottom. Strain the juice into a small saucepan and let reduce over low heat to about ⅔ cups. Skim the fat from the surface. Whisk the juices over low heat, adding the grated tonka bean, butter, and lemon juice.

Presentation

Brown the sesame seeds in a non-stick skillet. Toast the sunflower seeds in the same way.

Slice the meat, place on the serving platter with the vegetables arranged in a colorful ring around the edges, and spoon the juices over all. Decorate with the sesame and sunflower seeds.

* THE PROVENÇAL GARDEN includes a vast selection of squash, including, in winter, a large orange fleshed courge, resembling a pumpkin, but with a more pronounced flavor and a firmer texture. In this recipe, acorn squash or pumpkin can be substituted.

CHEF'S NOTE

Be very careful to always have enough water in the bottom of the roasting pan to prevent the brown bits from burning. These succulent brown bits contribute to the flavorful jus, or pan juices that make a natural sauce.

The Chef's Advice

USING AROMATIC HERBS

Certain plants can be used either fresh or dried, at least for common uses: thyme, bay leaf, sage, savory (called pèbre d'ail *in Provence), and oregano. The two forms are, nonetheless, two different things, because the same plant—sage, for example—can impart a totally different flavor depending upon whether it is dried or fresh.*

Proper storing is essential for aromatics: they should be protected from the air, light, and above all from humidity. Any humidity will quickly give a musty, mildewed taste. When buying dried herbs, it's important to know how old they are, because they can only be kept well for about six months.

Can different aromatic elements be combined in the same dish? Some of them yes, others, no. Don't marry basil and tarragon, for example, but basil and sage go well together. Thyme often dominates a dish. Nonetheless, certain dishes call for mixtures: particularly pizza, which needs intense, powerful flavors.

But in general, I prefer not to mix. When a lot of ingredients are mixed in a recipe, there are too many elements and the result is complicated. What's more, the aromatic herbs of the South of France have very strong flavors. In the Loire Valley or in Paris, it is undoubtedly easier to mix herbs since the flavors are less pronounced. It is the same in the South in winter when basil and chives grow in hot houses and have less flavor. In winter, I bring fresh herbs from Morocco, which allows me to find the same taste characteristics as in summer. If you don't have this possibility, in less sunny seasons, opt for herbs such as thyme, savory, rosemary and sage which will add a pleasant flavor to all your preparations.

HEALTH AND PLEASURE,

RIVIERA-STYLE, AROUND 1930

MEDITERRANEAN CUISINE IS TODAY CONSIDERED one of the healthiest in the world. It was not always so. In 1928, the French writer Colette, having recently settled into her villa *La Treille muscate* at Saint-Tropez, noted with amusement the behavior of the typical English tourist of the time, whom she overheard exclaiming, "This region would be delightful if only it were not so hot and the food were bearable!" Everywhere, Colette says, such a man "demanded steak and potatoes . . . no garlic, please! His stomach will not stand it and his doctor absolutely forbids olive oil!" The novelist herself tended a small vegetable garden that she watered at dawn, in the cool of the morning. In several books, she describes it lovingly as "decked out with vegetable graces" and regularly defends "the excellence of any simple Provençal dish, the virtues of garlic, the transcendence of olive oil." She remains loyal to "those three inseparable glossy vegetables, high in color and rich in flavor: the eggplant, the tomato and the sweet pepper!"

A few years later, another novelist, an Englishman but not a tourist, settled in the backcountry behind Nice. Ford Madox Ford had survived the trench warfare of World War I, described in a series of novels still considered the best of their kind. In the early 1930s he praised Provence as an Eden Garlic Garden and a pacifist's paradise. He had known the glitzy and glamorous Riviera of the Belle époque as a child, since one of his uncles regularly invited him to Monte Carlo. Then as a soldier, wounded at the front in 1917, he was sent to convalesce at Cap Martin where the locals provided these poor infantrymen with chauffeur-driven limousines, golf lessons, and the best wines and food. He also recounts a postwar experience when he was invited by affluent compatriots to sample "poached turbot in the style of the Princess of Wales!" He claims it made him sick for a week.

Ford chose to live like Colette, alternating work on his garden and on his books. He observes that "an almost purely vegetable diet varied

A small vegetable garden ensures regular harvesting at the peak of flavor.

with a little fish still characterizes the tables of the inhabitants of Provence today. So that their cuisine is rather picturesque than plutocratic . . ." He cites his own life as a model. "When I am at home [in the hills above Nice] I eat astonishingly little—so little that the Septentrional would hardly believe that on it I can get through a fairly grueling day of writing and gardening . . . for lunch a salad . . . for dinner about two ounces of veal or mutton . . . one vegetable from the garden—tomatoes, egg plants, *petit pois, pois-mangetout,* stringbeans, or sorrel and some stewed fruit or jam . . . Nevertheless I do not lose weight—which I put down to the olive oil and *fines herbes* which accompany or assist at that cuisine. For olive oil alone is a sufficient nutriment and *fines herbes* assist in the digestion of other foods."

Not everyone agreed. "My nearest neighbors are, on the one hand, a French seigneur of the *ancien regime* who is an Anglo-maniac . . . and on the left, a really scintillating American of about the rank of Duchess and of German extraction. . . . Both my friends use my garden path as a short cut to the high-road and come upon me at

my irrigation in the attire of the gone native. I hear a gentle sigh and at my back will be the French nobleman who insists that the Provençal cooking and life are those of savages. Let me take example by him and eat nothing but *boeuf saignant* without condiments and play a round of golf every morning! I suggest that he come and eat with me . . . We have today stuffed cabbage *à la Provençale*—as eaten by Cato in ancient Rome. He shudders and says: 'If I thought I should have to work in a garden at sixty, and eat anything *à la Provençale!*' . . . an appointment with his stomach-specialist will preclude his availing himself of my so amiable invitation . . . I return to my occupation of, with my hoe, leading the irrigation water from the melons to the petit pois. I hear a gentle sigh. Her charming Grace is behind me . . . she says: 'Of course no one but a lunatic would think of gardening in the South of France!' I say: 'Have a fig, Duchess . . .' She looks at my peas: 'I should have thought it was *wrong* to have peas so late in the year . . . But come and try my canned peas . . . '"

Ford continues, "Alas it *was* in the middle of the dog days. I had been up at five and dug till seven when I had had my coffee. I had irrigated till nine when those two martyrs to indigestion has come upon me . . . After that I had written till one—which is too long; had lunched off a tomato salad; taken my siesta; set out some romaine plants . . ."

Fashions have changed a good deal since Ford's time, in cuisine as in nutrition. Both of these authors were considered eccentric in their time but exemplify a happy and healthy lifestyle which inspires many imitators today.

Above and right: The vegetables of Provence, including zucchinis with their flowers, were not always appreciated as they are today.

Girolle mushroom salad
with fresh almonds and foie gras

For 4 servings:
— For the vegetables: 3 ounces (¾ cup) green beans, salt, 1 provençal "violin" [french word?] zucchini*, 1 pound *girolle* mushrooms**, 1 pinch coarse salt, 4 fresh almonds***, ¾ ounce black truffle
— For the vinaigrette: 1 teaspoon lemon juice, salt, pepper, 4 tablespoons olive oil, 1 teaspoon hazelnut oil, a few drops balsamic vinegar
— For the foie gras mousse: ¼ cup (2 ounces) whipping cream (preferably 35 percent fat or other reduced fat cream), salt, pepper, 2 teaspoons unflavored, powdered gelatin or 2 sheets, 3 ounces foie gras terrine****, 2 drops lemon juice or vinegar
— For the presentation: 10 petals of untreated roses or the leaves of small a belgian endive, a few drops olive oil, a few drops balsamic vinegar

The vegetables

Snap off the ends of the green beans and rinse. Cook in a large saucepan of boiling salted water (1½ tablespoons salt for 1 quart water) until just tender, then plunge them into cold water and drain immediately.

Cut the zucchini, unpeeled, into thin rounds and cook in boiling salted water as for the green beans, rinse and drain. The zucchini should be tender-crisp.

Trim the stem ends of the *girolles* and rinse four or five times. Add 1 tablespoon water and the coarse salt to a saucepan with the *girolles*. Cover and cook for 2 minutes over high heat; the *girolles* will shrink a little. Drain thoroughly and refrigerate.

Crack open the almond shells, remove the fresh almonds, and peel away the inner membrane. Slice thinly. Peel the truffle, reserving the peelings for the foie gras. Slice the truffle thinly, set aside.

The vinaigrette

Mix the lemon juice with a little salt and pepper. Incorporate the olive oil, whisking constantly, followed by the hazelnut oil and the balsamic vinegar.

The foie gras mousse

Whip the cream to soft peaks, and season lightly with salt and pepper. Soften the gelatin in a little warm water. Soften the foie gras over low heat in a small saucepan, working it gently with a spatula until creamy and warm, but not melted. Add the gelatin to the warm foie gras, incorporating it well. Delicately fold in the whipped cream. Add the truffle peelings, finely chopped, and the lemon juice or vinegar. Chill in the refrigerator for about 1 hour.

Presentation

Season the *girolles*, the green beans, and the squash separately with a little vinaigrette. Fan the zucchini out on the plate, top with a pyramid of green beans, and arrange the *girolles* in the center. Using a spoon, form the foie gras into neat ovals or *quenelles* and place on top of the vegetables. Top with a few thin slices of truffle.

Decorate with the rose petals. Drizzle a few drops of olive oil on each petal, followed by a drop of balsamic vinegar. Sprinkle with the fresh almond slices.

Serve the salad very cold, seasoned just before serving, so that the vegetables remain crisp.

* VIOLIN ZUCCHINI *is another product of the bounty of Provençal squash. It resembles the ordinary zucchini, but is pale rather than dark green in color, and has a distinctive violin shape with one end larger and rounder than the other. If not available, ordinary zucchini can be substituted.*

** GIROLLES: *This trumpet-shaped wild mushroom is in the same family as chanterelles, but is larger, firmer, and ranges from yellow to yellow-orange in color. If fresh girolles are not available, substitute cultivated white mushrooms.*

*** *Fresh almonds, widely used in French cooking, have a mild milky flavor and a softer texture than dried toasted almonds.*

**** *Foie gras terrine: The best for this recipe is fresh duck or goose foie gras that has cooked gently in a terrine, or semi-conserved foie gras usually sold in glass jars.*

CHEF'S NOTE

Choose small girolles; *they will cook more quickly while still remaining firm. If fresh almonds are unavailable, substitute slivered almonds cooked for 2 minutes in a little cream flavored with a drop of amaretto (almond liqueur).*

Pheasant hen
with walnuts, truffles, and pomegranate seeds

FOR 4 SERVINGS :
— FOR THE PHEASANT: 2 PHEASANT HENS (2½ POUNDS EACH) WITH THEIR LIVERS, SALT, PEPPER, ¼ CUP OLIVE OIL
— FOR THE SAUCE: 2 SHALLOTS, 1 CARROT, 1 SLICE CELERY ROOT (1¼ OUNCES), 1 CLOVE GARLIC, 2 STEMS DRIED FENNEL, 1 SPRIG THYME, ½ BAY LEAF, 3 JUNIPER BERRIES, 4 SLICES DRIED CÈPE MUSHROOMS, ¼ CUP MARC DE PROVENCE*, SCANT ½ CUP DRY WHITE WINE, 1 TABLESPOON OLIVE OIL, 1¼ OUNCES FOIE GRAS TERRINE**, 1 TABLE-SPOON WALNUT OIL, 1 OUNCE BLACK TRUFFLE
— FOR THE *PAIN PERDU****: ⅓ CUP PLUS 2 TABLESPOONS CREAM, 1 OUNCE BLACK TRUFFLE, SLICED (RESERVE PART FOR THE PRESENTATION), 2 SLICES FIRM SANDWICH BREAD, 1½ TABLESPOONS UNSALTED BUTTER, 2 EGGS, SALT, PEPPER
— FOR THE PRESENTATION: 1½ TABLESPOONS UNSALTED BUTTER, 12 SHELLED FRESH WALNUTS, 1 POMEGRANATE, RESERVED BLACK TRUFFLE SLICES

The pheasant

Preheat the oven to 425°F. Season the pheasants with salt and pepper and truss them. Brown on all sides in the olive oil in a roasting pan. When the skin is nicely browned, place in the preheated oven and roast for 14 minutes. Transfer to a rack, cover with aluminum foil, and let rest in a warm oven (turned off). When the pheasants are cool enough to handle, separate the thighs and breasts (with the breast bone) from the carcasses.

The sauce

Break up the carcasses and return them to the roasting pan. Peel and chop the shallots, carrot, and celery root, add to the pan and brown with the carcasses. Peel and crush the garlic and add to the roasting pan with the dried fennel, thyme, bay leaf, juniper berries, and dried cèpes. Flame with 3 tablespoons of the marc de Provence, add the white wine and a scant ½ cup water. Add the pheasant thighs and cook in the juices for 25 minutes.

Strain the cooking juices into a saucepan, skim off any fat from the surface, and let reduce over low heat to about ½ cup.

Sauté the pheasant livers with the olive oil in a skillet. When cooked through, process to a fine purée with the foie gras. Incorporate about a fourth of this mixture into the sauce, whisking. Add the remaining tablespoon marc de Provence to the sauce and strain through a fine sieve. Whisk in the walnut oil. Just before serving, reheat the sauce and add the truffle, thinly sliced.

The pain perdu

Debone the pheasant thighs, chop them finely, and combine with the remaining liver/foie gras mixture, the cream, 1 tablespoon of the sauce and a few of the truffle slices. Cut the bread slices, crusts removed, into small cubes. Brown them in a skillet with 2 teaspoons butter, and add to the pheasant and foie gras mixture, along with the beaten eggs, salt, and pepper. Melt the remaining butter in a skillet about 7 inches in diameter. Add the mixture and cook over low heat as for a flat omelette. Invert on a plate and cut into quarters.

Presentation

Preheat the oven to 350°F. Before serving, heat the pheasant breasts in a baking dish with the butter for 10 minutes. Using a pointed knife, remove the breasts from the bone. Remove the membrane from the fresh walnuts. Cut open the pomegranate and separate the seeds.

Place one quarter of the *pain perdu* on each serving plate. Top each with ½ pheasant breast. Sprinkle the pomegranate seeds and fresh walnuts around the edges of each plate. Spoon the sauce over and garnish with truffle slices.

* MARC DE PROVENCE *is white brandy from Provence. Subtitute any good quality brandy, preferably clear.*

** FOIE GRAS TERRINE: *The best for this recipe is fresh duck or goose foie gras that has cooked gently in a terrine, or a semi-conserved foie gras usually sold in glass jars.*

*** PAIN PERDU *is generally translated in English as french toast, but the pain perdu in this recipe resembles a rich, savory bread pudding.*

CHEF'S NOTE

Replace the truffles with thin slices of cèpe or morel mushrooms sautéed in a little olive oil. The pain perdu *can also be poured into a buttered 7-inch cake pan and baked in the oven for 10 to 12 minutes at 400°F.*

Discovery and Adventure

«Art in Provence never forgets the earth from which it sprang, and its finest works, even those born in cities, never lose that rustic and refined air which confers nobility on our countryside . . .»

Max Pol Delavouet

THE COD EPIC

Gifts from the sea, so generous for centuries, are not inexhaustible.

ONGOING CONTROVERSY ABOUT ATLANTIC COD (*Gadus morhua*) reminds us that its history has long been global. The "King of the Sea" has been fished and traded between continents at least since the ninth century, when Vikings from Scandinavia discovered the shoals of the Grand Banks off the coast of Newfoundland. These fearless explorers were soon joined by fleets from Brittany and the Basque country. This was, of course, long before Columbus "discovered" America. And though fishermen were not advertising their finds, it was a secret too big to keep. In the following centuries, cod played a crucial role in several wars already of world status, like the Seven Years War involving Europe, North America, and Asia (1756–1763) or the American War of Independence in 1776. The New England climate was thought to favor better-quality cod than Canadian waters, and fish prospered there in such amazing abundance that one had only to scoop a basket through the water to catch them. The merchant elite of Boston went so far as to call itself the Cod Aristocracy. American fleets regularly sold cod to Mediterranean countries, to East Africa and in the Caribbean in exchange for salt, rum, and slaves. Cod became an integral part of Portuguese, Greek, Basque, Jamaican, Canadian, American, and Provençal cuisine. Mark Kurlansky, who tells this story in his book *Cod*, claims that between 1550 and 1750, cod supplied 60% of all the fish eaten in Europe. Cod is practically a miraculous fish. It has few parasites or diseases and breeds easily into the millions. But in spite of all these advantages, it has all but disappeared from the seas because of that formidable predator: humankind.

Provence was always one of New England's high-quality markets. The cod consumed in small hill towns in Provence in the eighteenth century came through Aigues-Mortes, Marseille or Hyères, brought by brigs and schooners from Canada or the U.S., come to sell their catch and return home with their holds full of salt. Inland consumers treasured

dried and salted cod for the many lean days of the Christian calendar when meat was forbidden, so much so that religious communities sometimes joined together to place their orders for large quantities. Other fish—anchovies, tuna, and sardines for example—were also salted and spread out on racks on the beaches, then sold at the open-air markets. Did the family cooks miles inland realize that their cod came from far more distant shores than their sardines? It was cod, at any rate, that played a major role in rural ceremonies such as the Christmas Eve feast called the *gros souper* (cod with leeks, cod in red wine sauce). In the traditional nativity scenes displayed in every Provençal household at this season, where *santons* (little saints) bring offerings to Baby Jesus, cod often counts among the important gifts. Later on, when great open-air banquets were held on important occasions (like American barbecue) the favorite fare was *aïoli*: mountains of cod and vegetables served with oceans of garlic mayonnaise. Today these dishes are appreciated all over the world along with the brandade of the Gard region (a blend of shredded fish and olive oil). In Nice, Norwegian "stockfisch—unsalted fish which

In French fresh cod is called cabillau; *once dried and salted, it becomes* morue.

Bouillabaisse is legendary in Provence and the subject of hot debate.

could also be haddock—is served with black olives, onions, and tomatoes in what has become a classic mixture. Dried on stakes outdoors, stockfisch was once used as currency by Scandinavian sailors.

For generations, cod provided good, cheap fare for families with limited budgets. Once modern comforts became commonplace in the twentieth century, housewives discovered an ingenious way of soaking the fish by placing it in the upper storage tanks of the old-style WCs: fresh, clean water rinsed it at every flushing! Provençal culinary historian René Jouveau remembers a hunter's way of preparing salt cod *à la matrasso* without previous soaking: with vinegar and garlic and potatoes baked in the ashes over a wood fire. But cod also had moments of glory. The same historian tells the tale of a dinner with the renowned gastronome Curnonsky in which cod, prepared in five different ways, was revered by the great chef.

Cod contains only 3% fat and as much as 80% protein. For this reason, the Renaissance cook Taillevent judged that dried cod especially needed preparations with added fat. Every part of the fish is edible: its innards, its tongue, and its cheeks count among the most prized parts in some countries. Jacques Chibois loves to experiment with this fish, preparing it as a stuffing for tiny ravioli, or in a salad inspired by the classic Nimes brandade—without potatoes added, enriched only with cream and olive oil and accompanied by tomatoes and lettuce and a lemon vinaigrette. He also adds cod to enrich other fish or vegetable dishes, for a little added flavor. In spite of its new status as a rare luxury item, cod still stimulates the imagination, not least because its salty tang recalls such a fabulous history of travel and adventure.

Cod in coarse salt
with fork-mashed potatoes and pearls of beet vinaigrette

FOR 4 SERVINGS:
— FOR THE COD: 1 CODFISH TAIL (ABOUT 3 POUNDS), 2¾ POUNDS COARSE SALT, ½ CUP GRANULATED SUGAR, 1 BAY LEAF, 10 JUNIPER BERRIES, 10 BLACK PEPPERCORNS, ½ CUP MILK, FINE SALT
— FOR THE MASHED POTATOES: 1¼ POUNDS POTATOES (PREFERABLY MONALISA OR OTHER ALL-PURPOSE POTATOES), 5 TABLESPOONS OLIVE OIL, 1¼ OUNCES PITTED BLACK OLIVES, SALT
— FOR THE SAUCES: 1 COOKED BEET, ZESTS OF 3 UNTREATED LEMONS, SALT, PEPPER, 1 SHALLOT, ⅔ CUP OLIVE OIL, 1 TEASPOON SZECHUAN PEPPER, A FEW DROPS LEMON JUICE, 1 TEASPOON CHOPPED CHIVES, 1 TEASPOON CHOPPED BASIL
— FOR THE PRESENTATION: JUICE OF 1 LEMON, 8 CHIVES

The cod

Ask your fishmonger to bone the cod tail, separating it into two fillets, leaving the skin on. Place the fillets side by side, skin-side up, in a deep dish. In a mixing bowl, combine the coarse salt, sugar, bay leaf, juniper berries, and peppercorns. Cover the cod fillets with this mixture and refrigerate overnight.

Remove the fish from the salt (reserving the aromatics), brush off excess salt and place the fillets in a deep dish. Add enough water to cover and refrigerate for 6 hours. Change the water, and return to the refrigerator to de-salt for 6 hours longer. Drain the fillets and cut into thick, even slices. Combine the milk with 4 cups water in a saucepan and bring to a boil. Add a pinch of fine salt, and the reserved aromatics (bay leaf, juniper berries, and peppercorns). Add the cod and poach in the warm liquid for 10 minutes, then remove from the heat.

The potatoes

Peel the potatoes and cook in a saucepan of boiling salted water (1½ table-spoons for 1 quart water) for 20 to 30 minutes, depending upon the size, until tender. Drain, then mash with a fork or in a mortar and pestle, incorporating the olive oil.

Blanch the olives in boiling water three or four times, drain and chop coarsely. Add the olives to the potatoes, then season to taste with salt.

The sauces

Peel the beet and process with the zest of 1 lemon, 1 tablespoon water, salt, and pepper. Strain to obtain a very fine pulp and set aside. For the second sauce, peel and chop the shallot and sauté in a skillet with 1 tablespoon of the olive oil. Add the finely chopped zests of 2 lemons, the remaining olive oil, the crushed Szechuan pepper, a few drops lemon juice, the chives, and the basil. Before serving, warm this sauce slightly.

Presentation

Just before serving, drain the cod fillets and sprinkle generously with lemon juice.

Spoon 4 tablespoons of the mashed potatoes in the center of each plate, top with a fillet of cod, and drizzle a little of the warm herb sauce on the plates, spooning some of the herbs and spices on top of each piece of cod. Add a few drops of the beet sauce to each plate and "marble" it by drawing the tip of a paring knife through the sauce to create a decorative effect. Decorate with 2 chives.

CHEF'S NOTE

To make this recipe a perfect success, warm the herb sauce briefly only at the last moment so that it retains all of the freshness and flavor of the herbs and spices that it contains.

The Chef's Advice

ABOUT SALT COD

There are numerous recipes, and particularly many traditional Provençal dishes, that are made with dried or salted cod. If you want to prepare the salted cod yourself, as I do, start with a generous pound of codfish, about 2 to 2½ inches thick. The fish needs to be entirely salted, as for a smoked salmon: 2¼ pounds salt, 1½ tablespoons sugar (absolutely necessary), and a little crushed juniper berry. The only thing left to do now is to cover the fish with this mixture and let it marinate for a day or two.

By this process, the salt and iodine penetrate the flesh and the salt partially cooks the fish. For this reason it is necessary to give it time to permeate to the very center of the fish and not to remove the salt until a day or two later. To do this, rinse the fish, then soak it in cold water for about a day (the time is a function of the thickness of the fish and the length of time it was left in the salt). Next, the fish can be poached.

Use the coarse salt of France's Camargue region, and by no means refined salt, nor the costly fleur de sel: *what a waste that would be.*

ALCHEMY AND MAGIC:

THE MAS DE LA BRUNE

A MERMAID STRUMS HER LUTE ON THE HIGH TURRET of the Mas de la Brune. She invites travelers to discover this fine Renaissance domain south of Avignon, recently embellished by two original creations: the Alchemy Gardens and the Botanical Garden of Magic Plants. These are the work of designers Arnaud Maurières and Éric Ossart, who also planned the gardens of the Cluny Museum of Medieval Artefacts in Paris, among many others.

Live willow hedging in the Botanical Garden of Magic plants.

Marie and Alain de Larouzière bought this charming small hotel in the mid-1990s. Abandoned market gardeners' fields—long rectangles bordered by tall cypress windbreaks—stretched behind the house. The Larouzières both come from landed gentry, vintners and farmers who are also at home in the art world. One of their children, a geologist, is scientific director at the Vulcania Center in the Auvergne, while another married the director of the Villa Medicis foundation in Rome. Marie and Alain wanted to make gardens that would transform this farming landscape into art while evoking the history of the place. Maurières et Ossart began work here in 1996. In their beautiful book *Paradise Gardens*, they explain, "A garden is a veritable initiation of all the senses. It can even lead you towards a sixth sense." At the Mas de la Brune, visitors enjoy a quest for knowledge as well as the pleasures of an original vision.

The gardens echo both medieval and Mediterranean traditions in their inextricable mix of beauty and practical use. The very layout incorporates ancient lore. The Botanical Garden of Magic Plants pays homage to folk medicine, whereas the Alchemy Gardens celebrate an elite esoteric science transmitted among scholars in the deepest secrecy. In the botanical gardens, the tallest specimens grow at each end of the long rectangle, forming miniature forest squares including cypresses, plane trees, and junipers. They are bordered by live willow hedging pruned into a diamond pattern, which makes them more mysterious,

The Black Work:
its pool and its oaks.

half-open but inaccessible. Towards the center are lower squares composed of fruit trees under-planted with wildflower meadows. In the heart of the garden are formal herb parterres on either side of a long pergola supporting some twenty-four different varieties of grape vine. In each section, plants bear labels giving ample information about their possible uses, both medicinal and magical.

Local tradition claims that Pierre Isnard, who built the Mas in 1572, was an alchemist, and certain symbolic details sculpted on the façade seem to confirm this. This was enough to inspire the Alchemy Gardens in the second long rectangle. Throughout, discreet panels explain to visitors that the search for the philosopher's stone was a quest which "led initiates from the dark to the light, from sleeping waters towards the refreshing spring of knowledge, from narrow enclosed paths towards radiance." Marie de Larouzière judges therefore that "alchemy is not at all in contradiction with Christian faith."

These concepts translate into very concrete design terms. The visitor moves through three large sections: the Black Work, the White, and the Red. Each one has its symbolic numbers, figures, materials, and multiple associations embodied in stone, water, and plants. The Black Work is a labyrinth of dark foliaged hornbeam hedging, opening onto a line of oaks. Its paths are of slate encrusted with lead inscriptions. This is the reign of Saturn and of the intelligence. The White Work is a seductive labyrinth with curving marble paths disappearing among a profusion of gaura, Madonna lilies, Iceberg roses and tall, silvery grasses (*Miscanthis sinensis*), all arranged around a pale, moon-faced

The White Work:
Iceberg roses, gauras,
and miscanthus.

If not picked,
artichokes produce
large thistle heads
opening to intense
violet flowers.

pool. The hedge here is made of evergreen elaeagnus with a soft, luminescent underleaf. This is the kingdom of Mercury, appealing to intuition and feeling. Those who aspire to true wisdom will move on, however, through the white flowered oleander hedge to the Red Work, where a sun pattern radiates into thirty-two rows of deep red Prestige de Bellegarde roses around a six-pointed star pool. Miniature pomegranates extend the flowering season and Red parfum ramblers add brilliant color even to the walls. This is the realm of the imagination. Its clarity opens the door to universality.

So it is that these gardens are ancient in their inspiration but contemporary in their conception. The two large rectangles will eventually be separated by a new cypress hedge. While this is growing, these unconventional designers decided to use white sheets hung out on a clothesline barrier! Sometimes they are allowed to float like giant handkerchiefs, sometimes they are gathered in the middle like theater curtains. Thus bound, they become phantasmagoric characters standing guard. Either way, they add a great deal to the graphics of the design.

Such whimsical finds are typical of the work of Ossart and Maurières: simple and elegant but meeting the need at hand. The garden is full of such discoveries, and can also be experienced as a giant board game full of surprises. A third garden was recently added to these two, a labyrinth of silvery eleagnus stretches out in a band near the entrance. Seen from above, its meanders spell out the first word of the Bible in Hebrew: Bereshit. Nearby, a small, shady terrace welcomes visitors who want to experience alchemy and magic in the form of non-alcoholic cocktails that mix fruit juice with floral essences. Here it is also possible to ask questions, aided further in the unquenchable quest for knowledge by helpful expert guides, who are often the owners themselves.

French toast with roasted apples

For 4 servings:
— For the French toast: 4 slices of firm white sandwich bread, 5½ tablespoons unsalted butter, ½ vanilla bean, 1½ tablespoons granulated sugar, ½ cup milk, 2 egg yolks, 3 whole eggs
— For the sabayon: 5 egg yolks, 1½ tablespoons granulated sugar, 5 tablespoons softened unsalted butter, 1½ tablespoons Port, 1½ tablespoons Sauternes, 2 teaspoons liquid vanilla
— For the caramel: 6½ tablespoons sugar, ⅔ cup cream, ¼ cup truffle juice, 1 ounce truffle (¼ ounce chopped finely and ¾ ounce thinly sliced for the presentation)
— For the roast apples: 2 large golden delicious apples, 1½ tablespoons unsalted butter

The French toast

Preheat the oven to 350°F. Cut the bread, crusts removed, into cubes and sauté in the butter in a skillet until browned. Scrape the seeds from the vanilla bean, rubbing the seeds and bean pod with the sugar in a bowl. Warm the milk in a small saucepan, add the vanilla-sugar and let infuse. Remove the bean pod. Whisk the yolks and whole eggs together in a bowl. Pour the warm milk onto this mixture, stirring. Add the bread. Pour the mixture into a buttered baking dish. Bake in the oven for 35 minutes.

The sabayon

Whisk the egg yolks and sugar together in bowl held over a saucepan of boiling water (or in a double boiler). Continue whisking over the water until the mixture becomes foamy and firm. Whisk in the softened butter, Port, Sauternes, and liquid vanilla. Remove from the heat.

The caramel

Heat the sugar with ¼ cup water. When light brown, remove from the heat and stir in the cream. Add the truffle juice and the chopped truffles. Set aside.

The roasted apples

Peel and core the apples and cut into wedges. Sauté in a nonstick skillet with the butter turning the apples frequently until browned.

Presentation

Using an oval cookie cutter or a sharp knife, cut the French toast into 3-inch long ovals, placing one on each plate. Arrange the apple wedges on the toasts, drizzle the caramel over, and spoon a ribbon of the sabayon around each serving. Decorate with the thinly sliced truffles.

CHEF'S NOTE

Split the vanilla bean in half lengthwise, then rub it with the sugar to separate the tiny black seeds nestled in the bean pod. The sugar will, in this way, absorb all of the flavors of the vanilla.

Wild duck with quince,
dates, and tagliatelles of crisp celery root

FOR 4 SERVINGS:
— FOR THE DUCKS: 2 WILD MALLARD DUCKS WITH THEIR LIVERS, SALT, PEPPER, 1 TABLESPOON OLIVE OIL
— FOR THE SAUCE: 2 SHALLOTS, 1 CARROT, 1 OUNCE (1 SLICE) CELERY ROOT, 2 CLOVES GARLIC, 2 SPRIGS DRIED FENNEL, 1 SPRIG THYME, 1 BAY LEAF, ¼ CUP MARC DE PROVENCE*, SCANT ½ CUP TANNIC RED WINE (RED BANDOL, FOR EXAMPLE), 1 PINCH GRATED NUTMEG, 1½ TABLESPOONS UNSALTED BUTTER, 1½ TABLESPOONS OLIVE OIL, SALT, PEPPER, 1 OUNCE COOKED RED BEET, A FEW DROPS LEMON JUICE
— FOR THE FRUIT: 4 QUINCE, 2 TEASPOONS RED WINE VINEGAR, 2 TABLESPOONS HONEY, 1 TEASPOON CRUSHED *MIGNONETTE* PEPPER**, 2 JUNIPER BERRIES, 1 PINCH SUGAR, 1 POUND CELERY ROOT, 1½ TABLESPOONS OLIVE OIL, SALT, PEPPER, 16 DATES, 1½ TABLESPOONS UNSALTED BUTTER
— FOR THE PRESENTATION: 1 TEASPOON *MIGNONETTE*** PEPPER

The wild ducks

Preheat the oven to 425°F. Clean the ducks, reserving the livers. Season each inside and out with salt and pepper, and truss them. Place them on a hot roasting pan brushed with the olive oil and cook in the oven (or over medium heat on top of the stove) for 12 to 15 minutes. Transfer the ducks to a rack, cover with aluminum foil, and let rest in the warm oven (turned off).

When the ducks are cool enough to handle, separate the legs and the breasts (with breast bone) from the carcasses. Cover breasts and set aside on a rack while preparing the sauce with the legs.

Before serving, warm the breasts in a 350°F oven for 5 to 8 minutes, then remove the fillets from the breast bones using a sharp knife. Season with salt and pepper.

The sauce

Peel and chop the shallots, carrot, and celery root. Peel and crush the garlic. Break up the duck carcasses, return them to the roasting pan and brown with the shallots, carrot, and celery root. Add the garlic, fennel sprigs, thyme, and bay leaf. When well browned, add the duck legs. Flame with the marc de Provence, add the red wine and 3½ cups water. Cook for 45 minutes over very low heat.

Remove the duck legs and set them aside. Strain the cooking liquid into a small

saucepan and simmer over low heat until reduced to about ⅔ cup. Add the nutmeg. Whisk the sauce incorporating the butter and olive oil. Season with salt and pepper.

Process the beet to a purée and add 1 tablespoon to the sauce. Just before serving, add the lemon juice.

The fruit and tagliatelles

Peel the quince, removing core and seeds, and cut into wedges. Place in a saucepan with 1 teaspoon red wine vinegar, the honey, crushed peppercorns, crushed juniper berries, a pinch of sugar and 1 cup water. Cover and cook over low heat for 45 minutes. At the end of the cooking, remove the cover and reduce over low heat until cooking juices thicken enough to coat the quince wedges.

Peel the celery root and slice as thinly as possible, about 1/16-inch thick. Trim the slices into tagliatelles strips, about ⅜-inch wide. Season with salt and pepper. Place in a non-stick skillet with the olive oil and sauté quickly over high heat, stirring constantly until nicely browned.

Just before serving, cut the dates in half, remove the pits, and sauté in a skillet with the butter. Deglaze with the remaining 1 teaspoon of the red wine vinegar.

Presentation

Arrange the celery root tagliatelles on the serving plates, and top with the duck breasts. Arrange the quince wedges and dates harmoniously around the plates. Position the duck legs at an angle with the breast and wings (see photo), and spoon the sauce over. Sprinkle with freshly crushed mignonette pepper.

* MARC DE PROVENCE *is white or clear brandy from Provence. Subtitute any good quality brandy, preferably clear.*

** MIGNONETTE PEPPER: *Crushed or coarsely ground black peppercorns*

CHEF'S NOTE

Select plump dates of the best quality.

The Chef's Advice

WINTER FRUITS

It is always best to cook with the fruits of the season at hand. In winter, we have citrus fruits and kiwi, both already well known. The feijoa, very fragrant, also ripens in France. I also like kakis or persimmons, the fruit of a tree called a plaqueminier *in French. I prefer what we call* kakis-pommes, *a grafted variety that is not only larger and fleshier, but it also keeps better (it holds its shape and doesn't become "stringy"). Persimmons, like kiwi and* nèfles, *pear-shaped fruits of the medlar tree, are fruits that should be picked before the frost to allow them to ripen slowly on racks. I also love the exotic fruits that ripen in the Southern hemisphere during our winter. I have a weakness for mangos, passion fruit, papayas and coconuts. The pineapple has an exceptional aroma and can be combined with many other fruits such as apples, bananas, coconut and mangos. Thanks to its acidity, it serves as a counterpoint to other flavors. I like the little pineapples of the Reunion Island, as well as tiny little bananas that are full of flavor. When choosing exotic fruits, it is important to first know if they were shipped by air or by boat. In the first case, the fruit ripened where it grew. On the other hand, if they were transported by boat, they were picked green and ripened in refrigerators. In addition, some fruits have different ripening seasons according to their origin; the mango season, for example, isn't the same in Brazil as it is in Asia or Africa. To choose well, it is important to know where the fruit comes from and its ripening season. The best approach is to inform yourself, either through your own research or by asking a truly professional fruit and vegetable dealer.*

A TRUFFLE REVIVAL
ON THE RIVIERA

T HE KNOBBY BLACK FUNGUS KNOWN AS THE PERIGORD TRUFFLE is world famous. But not everyone knows that 80% of the French harvest, including many truffles sold under the Perigord label, comes from Provence. The markets of Richerenches in the Drome department, Carpentras in the Vaucluse, and Aups in the Var lead the field. Now there is a new competitor: truffles from the Riviera. In the department of the Alpes-Maritimes, Michel Santinelli, working for the Chamber of Agriculture, has been inseminating neglected fields and wasteland with truffle spores for the last ten years. This is the department's secret weapon for protecting abandoned farmland from the dangers of forest fires and real estate speculation. The Union of Black Truffle Producers of the Alpes-Maritimes, under Santinelli's direction, takes charge of training, advising, experimenting, and conducting technical surveys as well as coordinating private orders for inseminated trees and group plantings. Once a year, in January, a Truffle Fair is held at the Bastide Saint Antoine. Small producers can sell their harvest here directly to consumers at a decent price.

Jacques Chibois has been Santinelli's accomplice in this effort from the start. Santinelli explains, "You know, when people talk about truffles, there is often a sly look, a suspicion of trickery. Our aim is to educate the consumer and teach him or her that with just twenty or thirty euros, you can make a dish for three or four people that lets everyone share the pleasure of fresh truffles." The Fair also welcomes cheese makers, honey, and jam vendors and even a man who cooks snails—all listed with the *Mutualité sociale agricole* as farmers. For this event, Jacques Chibois prepares lunch for some 400 people (prior registration required).

Santinelli and Chibois together imagined these festivities about ten years ago. The truffle expert respects his friend's constant desire to understand and experiment with food. "Give him a basket of truffles with only one Chinese intruder among them [a species of similar

appearance but little flavor] and he will winkle it out right away!" remarks Santinelli. Truffles inspire Chibois to create the culinary mixtures he most enjoys, using various types of produce that ripen at the same time. Truffles blend well, for example, with root vegetables.

Are Riviera truffles as good as those from other regions? Chibois, born and bred in the southwest, swears they are. *Tuber melanosporum* is a strange genus which consists of a single species, rather capricious, thriving only under very specific conditions. To encourage it, one must create, or re-create, the proper setting, including alkaline soil not too packed down with enough humus to provide a rich microscopic life. Locally, flavors obtained may vary considerably according to the amount of sun or shade, soil quality, the species of tree serving as host and the surrounding vegetation. But from region to region, Santinelli maintains, the average quality of the truffle remains invariable. Differences in the rate of maturing can affect taste, he adds. All truffles begin in the spring at about the same time and all grow big at the same time, in mid August, but after that their ripening can vary a good deal. Harvesting takes place from late November through late February. Mature truffles have dark skin while the flesh shifts from reddish to white to black with definite veins.

Truffles are not new on the Riviera, since Roman historians already mention them here. But when farming all but disappeared in this region, so did the truffles. Today they are coming back in strength. In ten years, in this part of the world where every inch of land is precious, nearly 200 acres have become truffle grounds. The Union of

Buried treasure at the foot of a tree, truffles are dug up and sold at the Fair of the Bastide Saint Antoine.

Black Truffle Producers has met with great success and even obtained government sponsorship. The township of Le Rouret offered space for experimentation with planting, irrigation, pruning, and so on, in the hopes of providing better information to the public for the expansion of this cottage industry.

Michel Santinelli reminds aficionados that the truffle is naturally organic produce that cannot thrive in a laboratory or greenhouse. It is highly sensitive to drought and frost, and these factors can halve or double a year's production. Santinelli, who is also a hunter, knows that the truffle's main enemy is the wild boar, which can reduce a truffle ground to pulp overnight. And of course it takes about ten years from the time of first planting to first harvest. This alone discourages those whose main concern is fast profit. The quest for black diamonds is for Michel Santinelli a whole way of life. "The great mistake is to be in a hurry," he says. "You must never rush." For those who follow his example, truffle hunting offers a way of exploring the world, the earth, and one's own self.

Creamy truffle soup

For 4 servings:
— For the soup: 2 shallots, 2 tablespoons unsalted butter, 2 tablespoons dry white wine, 2 tablespoons Noilly Prat or other dry white vermouth, 7 ounces fresh white mushrooms, ¼ cup plus 2 tablespoons cream, pinch powdered poultry bouillon, ½ tablespoon red Port wine, a few drops lemon juice, salt, pepper, 1½ ounces finely chopped black truffle
— For the presentation: 4 slices baguette or country bread, 1½ ounces thinly sliced black truffle, fleur de sel*, freshly ground black pepper

The soup

Peel and chop the shallots and sweat them in a saucepan with the butter. Add the white wine and Noilly Prat vermouth, reduce for 2 minutes. Rinse and chop the mushrooms and add to the saucepan. Stir in 1¼ cups water, the cream, and powdered bouillon. Bring to a boil, cover, and cook for 5 minutes over low heat.

Process the mixture as finely as possible. Return to the saucepan and bring back to a boil. Add the Port, lemon juice, salt, and pepper. Stir in the chopped truffle.

Presentation

Toast the bread. Arrange some of the truffle slices on the toast, sprinkle with sea salt and finely ground pepper. Pour the soup into small warm bowls, sprinkle with the remaining truffle slices and freshly ground pepper.

* Fleur de sel, *the finest (and most costly) natural French sea salt, has a distinctive flavor.*

CHEF'S NOTE

Select firm, very white mushrooms to give the soup a lovely creamy color.

Chickpea purée,
soft-cooked egg with truffle cream

For 4 servings:
— For the creamy yolks: 3½ tablespoons unsalted butter, ½ cup plus 2 tablespoons cream, salt, pepper, 8 egg yolks, ⅓ ounce black truffle
— For the chickpea purée: 1¼ cups chickpea flour, salt, pepper, 6 tablespoons olive oil, 1½ tablespoons unsalted butter, ½ ounce chopped black truffle, 2 teaspoons grated Parmesan cheese
— For the truffle cream: 1 tablespoon (½ ounce) powdered veal stock, ⅓ ounce chopped black truffle, 2 tablespoons olive oil, salt, pepper, ½ to 1 tablespoon unsalted butter
— For the presentation: 4 egg shells, ⅓ ounce black truffle

The creamy yolks
Combine the butter and cream in a small saucepan with a pinch of salt and pepper, and bring to a boil. Pour this mixture slowly over the egg yolks, whisking constantly until very creamy. Add the truffle, thinly sliced.

The chickpea purée
Place the chickpea flour in a mixing bowl. Season with salt and pepper, and gradually add 2 cups water and the olive oil, stirring with a wooden spoon to obtain a smooth, slightly thick batter with the consistency of a crepe batter. Pour the mixture into a saucepan and warm over medium heat, whisking constantly. When the mixture begins to thicken, add the butter, chopped truffle and Parmesan. Carefully mix about half of the creamy yolk mixture into the chickpea purée.

The truffle cream

Combine ⅔ cup water with the powdered veal stock in a saucepan and bring to a boil. Add the truffle, olive oil, salt, and pepper. Process to obtain a very fine, smooth truffle juice, incorporating the butter at the last minute while continuing to process.

Presentation

Place a little of the chickpea purée in each shallow serving bowl. Pour a ribbon of the truffle cream around. Divide the remaining creamed yolk mixture among the 4 egg shells and place one in the center of each serving. Slice the truffle in fine julienne strips and sprinkle over each serving.

CHEF'S NOTE

Serve immediately to prevent the chickpea purée from thickening. If necessary, add a little warm water to the purée to restore its smooth texture.

The Chef's Advice

COOKING WITH CREAM

In France, we always opt for what we call "fleurette cream" or liquid cream instead of thickened cream or crème fraîche, because it is lighter, containing some of the whey and has undergone no fermentation. Fermentation causes the elimination of certain elements and increases the fat content.

The two creams are not used for exactly the same purpose. Personally, I recommend cooking almost exclusively with liquid cream. Thickened cream can be used to add a touch of acidity to whipped cream or to pastry cream, for example. However, be careful not to boil thickened cream because of the ferments it contains. Liquid cream, on the other hand, can be boiled like milk without taking on an acidic taste.

If you want to thicken a cream sauce with liquid cream, reduce the cream by evaporation. Of course this takes a little more time, but the sauce will be lighter and more flavorful. It is preferable to add a little lemon juice to the sauce at the end, rather than using a thickened cream that can be too tart.

Whatever cream you choose, use just a small amount in your dishes—only for certain fish, some soups and ice creams—and when possible, opt for light and flavorful liquid creams.

PAINTERS' GARDENS IN PROVENCE:

VAN GOGH, CÉZANNE, AND RENOIR

*Above right:
Each painter had
his favorite plants.
The olive trees like
"barbarian gods"
for Renoir, the iris
and cypress for
Van Gogh.*

ARTISTS HAVE BEEN INSPIRED by French Mediterranean landscapes since the Romantic movement of the early nineteenth century. Historian Françoise Cachin suggests that many of them perceived Provence "both as a hideaway and as a sort of readily accessible Paradise, which offered as well the pleasures of immediate sensation." Three celebrated post-Impressionists, Van Gogh, Cézanne, and Renoir, explored southern landscapes each in his own way. Each one also experienced a garden as a kind of refuge, combining sensuous seduction with an idealization of nature.

Van Gogh painted public parks in Arles between June and October of 1888, and described them in his letters as "brightened by beds of geraniums, orange in the distance under the black branches." Some of these experiments, says historian Ronald Pickvance, stressed "the commonplace and everyday, often with park benches and seated figures and a strong flavor of *la vie moderne*." But these favorite Arlesian promenades also inspired a series of four paintings on the theme Van Gogh called the "Poet's Garden." He imagined Dante, Petrarch, and Bocaccio walking among these shrubs on "shaggy carpets woven of flowers and greenery." This series was intended to become a decoration for Gaughin's room in the Yellow House and symbolized the Utopian community which Van Gogh hoped to found with his fellow painter in Arles. Hopes disappointed, alas, by the well-known disasters that followed. Today, the public gardens of the Place Lamartine, like the Yellow House itself, have disappeared, heavily bombarded during World War II because of their proximity to the railroad station. Visitors to Arles can still see the hospital courtyard parterres restored according to Van Gogh's depiction, or the cloister gardens of the Saint Paul asylum near Saint-Rémy, where the painter was later interned. But it was the public parks of Arles that inspired his most idyllic vision. A small remnant along the Boulevard des Lices still maintains the exotic trees and colorful bedding schemes of Van Gogh's time.

Cézanne's refuge was the studio he had built near Aix at Lauves in 1897. He loved to hunt for subjects outdoors in all weathers, *aller sur le motif*, as he called it, and thus he discovered this site. The existing house was torn down and rebuilt to provide an ideal studio made to the painter's exact specifications. Cézanne kept the gardener's shed and even the old gardener himself—a man named Vallier, subject of several portraits. The lot was described in the act of sale as a hunting ground. It included several terraces of old olive trees overgrown with pines, ash, beech, and oak, with colorful patches of wild lilac, Judas trees, wild plum, and cherry trees here and there. In the summer, bright spots were provided by pomegranates and geraniums cascading over the terrace walls, still visible in a series of water colors. When the writer Jules Borély visited Cézanne 1902, he described thus the panorama he could see from the house terrace. "Beyond this tangle of olive foliage and dry, dead trees, in the mauve light, the city of Aix sits amidst its surrounding hills, airy and cerulean," he wrote, adding, "Cézanne extended his arm to measure, between his thumb and forefinger, the cathedral spire." The painter may well have appreciated the volumes and disposition of his

terraced hillside which already suggested, by their compacted space, the foreshortening which would later lead to greater and greater abstraction. Today this landscape is entirely forested and the town has disappeared from view. But clearings in the wood are now used for temporary exhibits, thus allowing creative young people to experiment with new forms of land and nature art. Cézanne admired most in nature "her infinite variety," and his explorations are perpetuated still.

In 1907, Renoir bought his Riviera farm at les Colettes near Cagnes-sur-Mer. His aim was to save 148 ancient olive trees that a carnation grower wanted to cut down. Renoir compared these presences to "barbaric gods," according to his son Jean, who repeated the remark to historian Derek Fells. The painter had known this site for years as he too regularly explored the local countryside. It was his wife Aline who decided to build here in order to provide comfortable surroundings for her husband suffering more and more from rheumatoid arthritis. It was also she who imagined the garden. Renoir was at first mainly in-terested in her roses, grown for scent as well as looks.

Begun thus in 1908, the garden contained an abundance of single-flowered blossoms in lively colors including iris, ivy geraniums, and lavender. "Renoir only liked commonplace flowers," explained Aline to the sculptor Rodin when he came to visit. After 1912, the painter moved around the property in a wheelchair on paths designed for this purpose. Towards the end of his life, Renoir experienced his hillside more and more as Arcadian landscape that he portrayed on canvas as an evermore ideal union between man and nature. "The olive orchard," explains Derek Fells, "was for him a kind of wild garden, an idyllic setting."

If gardens play a minor part in the work of these three painters, they nonetheless were central in their lives, contributing for each to an idealizing vision. Van Gogh's was urban, while the other two preferred the unkempt vegetation of semi-wild hillsides. But these sites in Arles, Aix-en-Provence, and near Nice, each so different, have all witnessed a depth of experience and discovery that adds much to our perception of place in Provence today.

Above:
The Alpilles hills seen from the Saint-Sixte chapel in Eygalières.

Right: The Mont Sainte-Victoire, so beloved by Cézanne.

Hake with raisins
and caper flowers

FOR 4 SERVINGS:
— FOR THE SAUCE: 1¾ OUNCES *VINETTE** (OR 1 TABLESPOON RAISINS SOAKED IN *VERJUS**
OR CIDER VINEGAR), 1 SUGAR CUBE, 1½ TABLESPOONS UNSALTED BUTTER, ½ TABLE-
SPOON OLIVE OIL
— FOR THE PASTA: 5½ OUNCES *RISONI***, SALT, 1 PINCH TURMERIC, 1 PINCH POWDERED
POULTRY BOUILLON, ½ TABLESPOON OLIVE OIL, 2 TEASPOONS UNSALTED BUTTER,
1 SPRIG ROSEMARY, PEPPER
— FOR THE HAKE: 2 SMALL HAKE (1 TO 1-⅓ POUNDS EACH), FILLETED, SALT, PEPPER,
½ TABLESPOON OLIVE OIL
— PRESENTATION: 4 CAPER FLOWERS

The sauce

Rinse and pat dry the vinette (or the soaked raisins.) Place in a saucepan
with 2 cups water and simmer with the sugar cube for 2 hours over low
heat. Remove the vinette or raisins and set aside. Transfer a scant ½ cup
of the warm cooking liquid to a bowl and incorporate the butter and
olive oil gradually, whisking constantly.

The pasta

Cook the risoni for 12 minutes in a saucepan of boiling water seasoned
with salt, turmeric, and powdered poultry bouillon. Drain and let cool.
Just before serving, reheat the pasta in a saucepan with the olive oil, butter,
and rosemary. Taste and season, if necessary, with salt and pepper.

The hake

Season the hake fillets with salt and pepper, and cook in a nonstick skillet
with the olive oil over medium heat for about 3 minutes on each side.
Transfer the fish to a platter and let rest in a warm oven (turned off).

Presentation

Place a hake fillet on each serving dish, drizzle with the sauce and spoon
a little of the reserved vinette or raisins over each fillet. Sprinkle the
pasta around. Decorate with the caper flowers.

* VINETTE: *These tiny dried wild grapes have a distinctively tart taste. Substitute small
raisins soaked in* verjus, *the sour juice of unripe grapes, or in a little cider vinegar.*

** RISONI *is a tiny round pasta. If not available use another small pasta such as orzo.*

CHEF'S NOTE

*The caper flowers can by replaced
by nasturtiums. Cook the fish a
little in advance and let it rest
before reheating; it will hold up
better and have a firmer texture.*

Rock fish soup
with a symphony of mixed potatoes

FOR 4 SERVINGS:
— FOR THE BROTH: 2 ONIONS, 1 TABLESPOON OLIVE OIL, 4 CLOVES GARLIC, 3 SPRIGS DRIED FENNEL, A FEW FENNEL SEEDS, 4 CLOVES GARLIC, 1 BOUQUET GARNI (COMPOSED OF THYME, BAY LEAF, AND PARSLEY SPRIGS), 1 TABLESPOON TOMATO PASTE, 1 TOMATO, 1 TEASPOON SAFFRON THREADS, 5 BLACK PEPPERCORNS, 1 SMALL PINCH GROUND CAYENNE PEPPER, FISH BONES (OPTIONAL), COARSE SALT, FINE SALT, PEPPER
— FOR THE VEGETABLES: 12 SMALL *GRENAILLE** POTATOES, 4 *VITELOTTES**, SALT, PINCH SAFFRON THREADS, 7 OUNCES RAW BEET, 8 SMALL WHITE ONIONS
— FOR THE FISH: 3 POUNDS CLEANED, FRESH, ASSORTED MEDITERRANEAN-STYLE FISH SUCH AS RASCASSE (SCORPION FISH), *ROUGET* (RED MULLET), *DORADE* (SEA BREAM), *LOTTE* (MONKFISH), *SAINT PIERRE* (JOHN DORY), *LOUP* (EUROPEAN SEA BASS), SALT, PEPPER
— FOR THE PRESENTATION: 10 THIN SLICES MINI-BAGUETTE, 1 TABLESPOON OLIVE OIL, 1 OUNCE FRESH PARMESAN CHEESE

The broth

Peel and chop the onions, and sauté them in a large, deep sauté pan with the olive oil. Peel and crush the garlic cloves and add to the pan along with the dried fennel, fennel seeds, bouquet garni, and tomato paste. Chop the tomato and add it to the pan with 6 cups water, the saffron, peppercorns, Cayenne pepper, and fish bones (if available). Season lightly with coarse salt and cook for 20 minutes over low heat. Strain through a fine sieve, pressing the solids with the back of a spoon to squeeze out all of the juices. Return the broth to the pan. Correct seasoning.

The vegetables

Peel the potatoes, slice the *grenaille* into rounds and quarter the *vitelottes*. Place them in a large saucepan filled with boiling salted (1½ tablespoons salt to 1 quart water), season with the saffron threads, and cook for 10 to 18 minutes, depending upon the thickness of the slices and the varieties used; the potatoes should remain slightly firm. Drain. Plunge the beet in a saucepan filled with boiling salted water (1½ table-spoons salt to 1 quart water) and cook for 40 to 50 minutes. Drain, peel, and slice the beet.

Peel the onions. Just before serving, ladle a little of the fish broth into a small saucepan and cook the onions for about 8 minutes, then add to the broth.

The fish

Add all of the vegetables to the broth, place the fish on top of the vegetables. Season with salt and pepper. Cook for 5 minutes over low heat to poach the fish gently, removing from the heat shortly after the broth boils.

Presentation

Sauté the baguette slices in a lightly oiled, non-stick skillet.

Carefully remove the vegetables from pan and arrange in an attractive shallow serving bowl, top with the fish. Ladle the cooking broth over and top with thin curls of Parmesan, sliced with a vegetable peeler.

* Grenaille potatoes *are small, firm-fleshed waxy potatoes, with a pleasant nutty flavor. Substitute any other firm-fleshed variety.*

** Vitelottes *are small violet-colored potatoes, and can be substituted with other "exotic" potatoes.*

CHEF'S NOTE

Serve this fish soup with a rouille, a mayonnaise seasoned with 1 peeled, crushed clove garlic and a pinch saffron powder. Depending upon their size, the fish can be cooked whole or cut into thick slices. Or ask your fish monger to fillet the fish. In this case, keep the bones and heads for the broth.

The Chef's Advice

COOKING FISH

No matter how you decide to cook your fish, handle it gently because fish is very fragile, rich in water and albumin (a substance also found in egg whites). If fish is cooked too fast or at too high a temperature, the molecules explode, the water runs off, and all that remains is fiber. On the other hand, if cooked too slowly, the flesh contracts and the albumin turns into a milky residue with a very unpleasant order. Guard against temperature extremes: avoid cooking a very cold fish in a very hot skillet, the contrast will be too violent.

For each fish there's an appropriate cooking method. Red mullet is sautéed like a steak, above all when it is not too thick. John Dory and sea bream do not react well to violent cooking techniques: place them in a cold skillet with butter or oil and increase the temperature little by little, then cover and keep an eye of the cooking. With this method, the flesh remains very tender. If cooking a whole John Dory or sea bream, place the fish in a cold oven on a bed of fennel or herbs and increase the temperature progressively. Once cooked, the skin will crack a little, the fish will be rose à l'arête or pink at the bone, and the flesh will pull away from the bone easily.

For other fish in slices or fillets, sauté each piece, skin-side down, in a very hot skillet, long enough for them to caramelize, then remove from the heat. Set aside on a rack, and cover with aluminum foil. The residual warmth will gradually penetrate to the center, the albumin will coagulate while holding in the moisture. Hold the fish at about 85°F until just before serving. To serve, heat it for a few moments on the flesh side until it comes to ideal serving temperature of about 160°F. The same temperatures apply for a large oven-baked fish.

THE HERB AND FLOWER BUSINESS

Albert Vieille and Co. manages vast plantations of winter-flowering mimosa (Acacia dealbata)

AMONG THE MANY BUSINESSES PROCESSING FLOWERS that once existed in Grasse, Albert Vieille and Co. still stands out today. A thriving concern, it imports from forty countries worldwide to produce some 600 aromatic products—essential oils and waters, gums, solids, resins, and absolutes. It has even established a branch operation in Spain, called Aromasur, which distills and extracts the essences of local plants such as cistus, lavender, everlastings, thyme, and oregano. Albert Vieille's principal clients are perfumers and the cosmetic and food industries, as well as specialists in aromatherapy. In France, this company provides work for about thirty people, another eight in Spain. Its website (http://www.albertvieille.com) offers a wealth of botanical information, richly illustrated.

Albert Vieille and Co. combines in an exemplary manner international growth and regional roots. In 1920, this family business began by commercializing bitter orange peel (called coulanes locally). Albert Vieille, son-in-law of the founder, became general director of the company in 1968 at a time when many local processors were being bought up by multinationals. He built up the import side of the business while continuing the treatment of regional resources like jasmine, roses, orange blossoms, mimosa, violets, and iris. Georges Ferrando, Vieille's son-in-law and current president, developed the Spanish branch some years later. Close cousins, the Mul family, took charge of the growing and processing locally, while Jean-François Vieille, Albert's son, supervises the technical side.

Jean-François works his magic in Pégomas, in the family farmstead at the foot of the medieval citadel of Grasse. For jasmine, for example, the sequence begins with 7,000 hours of picking in the fields, counting one pound harvested per hour. The picked blossoms are processed in an old barn where four huge extractors reduce some 300 liters of flowers and the solvent in which they are macerated to thirty liters of precious nectar. Jean-François' laboratory occupies an outbuilding across the courtyard

The preparation of the floral harvest for treatment has always required patient attention.

and looks at first glance like a smallish modern kitchen. Instead of pots and pans, however, he has elegant glass stills and stainless-steel basins. Here, the natural wax of the petals is separated from the solvent used to capture it, the final step in the extraction. In yet another farm building, flowers are subjected to steam without solvent. The resulting liquid is separated into essential oil and scented waters (or *eaux*, as in *eau de Cologne*). The process is simple. Blossoms are packed into baskets through which the vapor moves, after which it is condensed. The lighter oils float on top. Lavender and rose flowers can also be thus treated, as much as three tons a day, as well as cornflowers from Bulgaria and witch hazel from the United States. Georges Ferrando sums up the basic principle: "Distillation is a highly natural phenomenon. When you raise your nose to the sky and see clouds going by, you are looking at the visible evidence of evaporation. And when you walk in dew-soaked grass in the morning, you are experiencing the condensation of the night."

Spread out all around the old farmstead are nearly 400 acres of fields brimming with roses and jasmine. On the hillside opposite are planted

EAU DE FLEURS D'ORANGER
SPÉCIALE
EXTRA CONCENTRÉE

CONTENANCE: 125 gr. D'EAU

NOUVEAU MODÈLE   DÉPOSÉ

PÉLISSIER-ARAGON
GRASSE, FRANCE

Above:
Albert Vieille and Co.
perpetuates a cottage
industry once wide-
spread in Grasse.

Right: Old bottles
of essence in the
Fragonard museum
in Grasse.

diagonal strips of silver leafed eucalyptus and the tree called mimosa in French (*Acacia dealbata*), which has bright-gold flowers in February. The river Siagne brings pure water from the Alps down to this land. The rose fields are striking, for the plants are pruned very low like vines in many parts of Provence, but with many very short root sprouts. The jasmine fields, laid out in long rows, are also treated in a characteristic manner: a strip only one yard long contains four or five plants, making roughly 25,000 per acre. The plants are shored up in winter like asparagus, and cut back to the ground after the harvest. The jasmine of Grasse is a special blend: *Jasminum grandiflorum* grafted onto roots of *Jasminum officinalis*. The shoots of the year are stretched on trellising in early summer, the blossoms picked between June and November. This is the method of production that has won for the jasmine of Grasse a controlled appellation label and given to its production a special sweetness (*une note confiturée* say the specialists) which distinguishes it from the exotic jasmines grown in Egypt or India.

Albert Vieille and Co. owes its survival to the support of Chanel Perfumes, now co-owner of the family property at Pergomas. Chanel insisted that processing take place as close as possible to the growing fields to avoid delays that might allow the flowers to ferment. Each day's harvest goes directly to the machines on arrival. In season, the pace is such that the technicians ask the women pickers to estimate as closely as possible the day's production, so they may foresee the quantities to be treated and the time to allow for extraction. Thus they can control both the quality of the flowers and of their transformation. Chanel buys the whole output of the jasmine production and has first option on the roses.

Albert Vieille and Co. is renowned in Grasse and beyond for the purity and quality of its products. As a wholesaler, it distributes its essences through the Lavoillotte family under the brand name of Solubarôme. This establishment sells the high-quality plant extracts used in cooking, such as the rose essence and orange flower water much appreciated by Jacques Chibois.

Chilled cherry soup
with linden flower syrup

For 6 servings:
— For the chilled cherries: 2¼ pounds fresh cherries (preferably dark or black cherries), 2 tablespoons honey (or ½ cup granulated sugar), 1 tablespoon vanilla sugar, ½ cup MARASQUIN* or other cherry liqueur
— For the linden flower syrup: 3 cups (1 bottle) sweet white wine, ¾ cup granulated sugar, 3½ ounces linden leaves and flowers
— For the presentation: 3 sprigs fresh cilantro, 5 sprigs fresh mint, linden leaves and flowers

The cherries

Rinse the cherries. In a large saucepan, melt the honey (or sugar) with 1 cup water and the vanilla sugar over low heat. Stir in the maraquin and the cherries. Bring to a boil and simmer for 3 minutes. Remove from the heat and let cool, then transfer to a large bowl. Refrigerate for 12 hours.

The linden syrup

Combine the wine and sugar in a saucepan and boil until the mixture becomes a little syrupy. Add the linden leaves and the juice from the chilled cherries. Bring to a boil again, remove from the heat and add the linden flowers. Let infuse.

As the mixture cools, taste the juice from time to time and remove the linden leaves and flowers when the syrup is flavored to taste. (The longer you leave the linden leaves and flowers, the stronger the taste will become.) Cover and refrigerate for 1 to 2 hours.

Presentation

Spoon the cherries into small serving bowls and spoon the linden syrup over them. Decorate with a little finely chopped mint and cilantro, or linden leaves and flowers.

* MARASQUIN: A maraschino cherry liqueur. It can be substituted with other cherry flavored liqueurs.

CHEF'S NOTE

Preparing this recipe with pitted cherries will make for a slightly more refined presentation, but the cherries will have a more authentic and pronounced flavor if you prepare them as above with the pits. In addition, the fruit will hold up better. Nonetheless, if you decide to use pitted cherries, bring them to a boil, but do not cook them in the juice.

FEASTS AMONG ROMAN RUINS

THE PONT DU GARD, a Roman remnant labeled a World Heritage Site by Unesco, rises in splendor between Nimes and Avignon. Its wild setting, carefully restored and fragrant with rosemary, welcomes visitors from all over the world. Nearby is a fascinating landscape conservatory called *Mémoire de garrigue* which illustrates the history of this site since Roman times—types of farming, rural architecture, wildflower meadows, and dry stone constructions, all beautifully explained.

The Pont du Gard was not a bridge but part of an aqueduct built over the Gardon River some 2,000 years ago. Its covered canal conveyed 20,000 tons of pure spring water every day in the direction of Nimes. The inner coating of this conduit still bears traces of a latex waterproof paint made by the Romans from fig juice, pork grease, and wine. The river far below can be violent—in 1958 it destroyed a modern suspension bridge downriver without affecting the Roman construction. In summer, however, its peaceful banks welcome bathers, hikers, and picnickers.

Many great writers have felt the power of this construction. In the sixteenth century, François Rabelais imagined his giant Gargantua building it as a game. Henry James judged it "unspeakably imposing." The French novelist Stendhal wrote, "Thyme, wild lavender, and juniper, all that grows in this wilderness, exhale their solitary perfumes here under a sky of dazzling serenity. For the hearts of the chosen, this monument is such an event that it must have the effect of sublime music." But if everyone pays homage to the undeniable beauty of the ruin, few think of food in its presence. With three notable exceptions.

The English writer Lawrence Durrell, in the novel *Quinx* which concludes his *Avignon Quintet*, imagined an elaborate feast given to celebrate the discovery of Templar treasure. This fictional "more than adequate buffet" was mounted between the arches of the Pont du Gard,

and the food was prepared by a chef from Nimes, called Tortoni, who "amidst a multiplicity of highly comestible cakes and pâtés had prepared the pedestal for the most important of his creations, a recumbent woman fashioned in butter, with trimmings uttered in caviar of several different provenances and helpings of *saumon fumé* and an archipelago of iced potato salad to round out the offering . . . the whole creation was offered in a disguised thermal showcase upheld by captious looking Cupids with sweet erections and honeyed grins."

Most meals taken on this site are infinitely simpler, more familial—and perhaps also tastier. Marcel Pagnol (author of *Manon of the Springs*) recalls many childhood picnics here. However, it was not food that led Marcel Pagnol's grandfather, a professional stonecutter, to bring his family to this site. "Whenever he had a day of leisure—that is, five or six times a year—he would take the whole family on a picnic some fifty yards from the Pont du Gard . . . While my grandmother was getting the meal ready and the children were splashing about in the river, he would climb onto the double platforms of this monument, take measurements, examine the joints, make surveys of cross-sections, fondle the stones. After lunch, he would sit down in the grass in front of the family seated in a semi-circle, facing that ancient Roman masterpiece, and gaze at it till nightfall. And that's the reason why, thirty years after, his sons and daughters, at the mere mention of the Pont du Gard, would raise their eyes to heaven and utter long groans," remembers Pagnol in *Memories of Childhood* (translation Rita Barisse, North Point Press 1986).

Curnonsky, baptized Prince of gastronomes in the mid twentieth-century, also ate by the Pont du Gard as a child, and his memories are succulent. "When summer vacation began, I was invited by my relatives in Uzes to join them for lunch on the banks of the Gardon. Late in the morning, a dilapidated coach took us to the Pont du Gard. My aunt Agnes as I recall wore quilted skirts and a flowery hat [. . .] my two cousins, Clémence and Éliane, were positively frothy with ribbons and ringlets, and I admired very much my uncle's broad felt hat and goatee which made him look like the poet Frédéric Mistral, who had the same tall stature.

Recently restored, the wild site of the Pont du Gard has been welcoming admirers for centuries.

"We passed by the château of the baron of Castille to arrive in front of the Pont du Gard, that solitary giant which stretches its golden arches etched against an azure sky to join two banks of grey boulders and dark evergreen vegetation . . . I found one day in my album of old yellowed photographs the following menu written in a fine hand, belonging to the nearby restaurant which often made us welcome. It is dated July 18, 1911 and the price given is three francs fifty. It was a pretty piece of seasonal cuisine from the Gard region. Among the hors d'oeuvres were picholine olives, cardoon hearts with anchovy butter, dried sausage from Anduze and truffle and cod turnovers (stuffed with *brandade* from Nimes). There were deep-fried little fish from the Grau and snails Languedoc style, teal from the Camargue on canapés served with curly endive *à l'aïllet é à l'oli d'oulivo* (with garlic and oil). Then *pélardon* from the nearby Cévennes (a delicious fresh cheese ripened in alcohol). Peaches from local farms and the crunchy almond biscuits of the Villaret. Wines from the Costières, Tavel et Clairette de Bellegarde. We stayed at table until nightfall . . ."

If restaurant prices have gone up, the pleasure of lunching opposite that golden bridge is much the same. Thanks to sensitive site restoration, the magic of Curnonksy's memories can be transmitted to future generations.

Red-clawed crayfish
and leek salad

For 4 servings:
— For the vegetables: 2 leeks, 3 tomatoes, 3 tablespoons olive oil, salt, pepper, 1 teaspoon zest of untreated lemon, ½ pound winter squash*, 1 pinch ground cinnamon
— For the crayfish: 5 cloves garlic, 3 onions, 1 rib celery, 4 dozen crayfish (in their shells), 3 tablespoons olive oil, 1 bunch thyme, 1 bay leaf, 1 rib celery, 3 tablespoons Cognac, 3 tablespoons dry white wine, salt, pepper
— For the sauce: 1 teaspoon balsamic vinegar, salt, pepper, 1 teaspoon tamari (Japanese soy sauce), 6½ tablespoons peanut oil, 2 tablespoons hazelnut oil, 2 tablespoons walnut oil
— For the presentation: 2½ cups (2 ounces) purslane** greens, a few drops olive oil, a few drops balsamic vinegar, 1 tablespoon clover flowers or other edible flowers

The vegetables

Trim the ends of the leeks, retaining a good amount of the pale green leaves and cut them lengthwise in quarters. Rinse thoroughly and drain. Dice into ¼-inch cubes. Cook for 5 minutes in a large saucepan of boiling salted water (1½ tablespoons salt to 1 quart water), then plunge them into cold water and drain immediately.

Preheat the oven to 275°F. Drop the tomatoes into a saucepan of boiling water for 2 minutes, and drain. Peel them, cut into quarters, and discard the seeds to make tomato "petals." Place the tomato petals on a baking sheet brushed with a little olive oil, season with salt and pepper and bake in the oven for about 2 hours until dried.

Dice the tomato petals, setting aside part of them for the presentation and mixing the rest with the leeks. Add 1 tablespoon olive oil, the grated lemon zest, salt and pepper. Peel the squash, cut into large rounds and then into 3 by ¼-inch matchsticks. Cook in a nonstick skillet with 1 tablespoon olive oil, salt, pepper, and cinnamon until cooked through, but still slightly firm.

The crayfish

Crush the garlic cloves in their skin. Peel and chop the onions and celery. Sauté the crayfish in a large sauté pan with the olive oil and garlic cloves. Add the onions, celery, thyme, and bay leaf. Flame with the cognac, and deglaze with the white wine. Add 2 cups water, season with salt and pepper. Bring to a boil and cook for 5 minutes. Remove the crayfish and drain. Reserve 8 crayfish with their heads (tail shell removed) for the presentation. Peel all of the remaining crayfish. Strain the cooking liquid into a saucepan, bring to a boil and reduce to about ½ cup.

Just before serving, coat all of the crayfish, including the 8 reserved for decoration, in the reduced cooking liquid.

The sauce

Combine the balsamic vinegar in a large bowl with a pinch of salt and pepper, and whisk in the tamari, peanut oil, hazelnut oil, and walnut oil.

Presentation

Arrange the squash in a fan on each plate. Place a band of leeks and tomatoes next to the squash, then top with the crayfish. Decorate each serving with two intertwined crayfish heads (see photo).

Rinse and thoroughly dry the purslane leaves and place a few leaves on the edge of each plate. Drizzle a drop of oil, then balsamic vinegar on each purslane leaf. Season the squash and the crayfish with about a tablespoon of the sauce.

Spoon a little of the reduced crayfish cooking liquid over each serving. Sprinkle the diced dried tomatoes on the crayfish and garnish with the clover flowers. Serve well chilled.

* THE PROVENÇAL GARDEN *includes a vast selection of squash, including, in winter, a large orange fleshed* courge, *resembling a pumpkin, but with a more pronounced flavor and a firmer texture. In this recipe, acorn squash or pumpkin could be substituted.*

** PURSLANE, *called* pourpier *in French, is a salad green or pot herb with thick, fleshy leaves. If not available, substitute other greens such as lamb's lettuce.*

CHEF'S NOTE

Clover flowers may be replaced by finely shredded radicchio leaves.

Langoustines with saffron, braised white beans, and tomatoes, and chayote squash

For 4 servings:
— For the vegetables: 3½ ounces (1 small) tomato, 2 new onions, 3 garlic cloves, 1 tablespoon olive oil, 1 small pinch ground cumin, 7 ounces shelled fresh white beans, 1 bouquet garni (1 sprig thyme, 1 bay leaf, a few sprigs parsley), 1 very pale chayote squash, 1½ tablespoons unsalted butter, salt, 5 leaves fresh basil
— For the langoustines: 12 large fresh langoustines, 6 tablespoons olive oil, 1½ tablespoons unsalted butter, 1 pinch saffron threads, salt, pepper

The vegetables

Drop the tomato into a saucepan of boiling water for about 2 minutes, drain, peel, and cut in quarters, scooping out the pulp and seeds over a bowl to catch the juices. Dice the flesh into even cubes. Strain the juices to remove the seeds.

Peel and chop the onions. Peel and crush the garlic. Brown the onions in a saucepan with the olive oil. Add the juice from the tomatoes, the garlic, cumin, beans, and bouquet garni. Add enough water to fill the pan by about half, bring to a boil, and cook over low heat for about 30 minutes.

Peel the chayote squash with a vegetable peeler, cut in half lengthwise, remove the core as for a pear, then slice into even wedges about ¼-inch thick. Cook in a nonstick skillet with the butter, a pinch of salt and 3 tablespoons water.

Just before serving, mince the basil and add to the chayote.

The langoustines

Remove the heads and shells from the langoustines, reserving 4 heads for the presentation.

Break up the heads and shells, and brown them in a sauté pan with 3 tablespoons of the olive oil. Add ¾ cup water and cook for 10 minutes. Strain the cooking juices through a fine sieve. Pour the juices into a saucepan with the cooked white beans, prepared in the preceding step. Add the butter, saffron, 2 tablespoons of the remaining olive oil, and the diced tomato. Season with salt and pepper and simmer for 3 minutes.

Season the langoustine tails with salt and pepper and cook in the remaining tablespoon olive oil in a nonstick skillet over high heat.

Presentation

Spoon about a tablespoon of the white beans onto each serving plate, then arrange three langoustine tails and one head in the center. Spoon the cooking juices from the beans over all and stand slices of the chayote squash between the langoustines.

CHEF'S NOTE

Choose a tomato of quality, plump and ripe. Add at the last minute, just before the beans boil so that the tomato retains its firmness and a touch of its acidity. If chayote squash is not available, replace it with slices of carrot.

Annexes

RECIPE INDEX

INDEX OF INGREDIENTS

ADDRESS BOOK

Jacques Chibois welcomes you at
La Bastide Saint-Antoine
48, avenue Henri-Dunant, 06130 Grasse
Tel: 33 (0)4 93 70 94 94   fax: 33 (0)4 93 70 94 95
www.jacques-chibois.com / info@jacques-chibois.com

The Provençal Home

What is a bastide?

Agence Emile Garcin
8, boulevard Mirabeau
13210 Saint-Rémy-de-Provence
Tel: 33(0)4 90 92 10 14   Fax: 33(0)4 90 92 49 72

Pavillon de Galon
84160 Cucuron
Tel: 33(0)4 90 77 24 15   Fax: 33(0)4 90 77 12 55
contact@pavillondegalon.com / www.pavillondegalon.com

Villa Saint-Louis
35, rue Henri-de-Savournin, 84160 Lourmarin
Tel: 33(0)4 90 68 39 18   Fax: 33(0)4 90 68 10 07.
villasaintlouis@wanadoo.fr
The two preceding establishments offer "chamber d'hôte" or bed and
breakfast of quality, but they are not open to the public for visits.

The pleasures of a Provençal brunch

In the footsteps of Nostradamus

Office de Tourisme / Tourist Office
Place Jean-Jaurès, 13210 Saint-Rémy-de-Provence
Tel: 33(0)4 90 92 05 22   Fax:33(0)4 90 92 38 52
www.saintremy-de-provence.com / tourisme.st.remy@wanadoo.fr

Office de Tourisme / Tourist Office
56, cours Gimon, 13300 Salon-de-Provence
Tel: 33(0)4 90 56 27 60   Fax: 33(0)4 90 56 77 09
ot.salon@visitprovence.com

Les Jardins de l'Alchimiste / The Alchemist's Gardens
Mas de la Brune, 13810 Eygalières
Tel: 33(0)4 90 90 67 77   Fax: 33(0)4 90 95 99 21
www.jardin-alchimiste.com / contact@jardin-alchimiste.com

Fine linens

Edith Mézard
Atelier de broderie / Embroidery Workshop / Château de l'Ange,
Lumières: 84220 Goult
Tel: 33(0)4 90 72 36 41   Fax 33(0)4 90 72 36 69

Michel Biehn
Magicien de maisons / The house magician
7, avenue des Quatre-Otages, 84800 L'Isle-sur-la-Sorgue
Tel: 33(0)4 90 20 89 04   Fax: 33(0)4 90 38 45 09

Musée Provençal du Costume et du Bijou /
Museum of Provençal Costume and Jewelry
2, rue Jean-Ossola, 06130 Grasse
Tel: 33(0)4 93 36 44 6   Fax: 33 (0)4 93 36 57 32
www.fragonard.com / fragonard@fragonard.com

A Provençal wedding

Bruno Gedda
Musical Stylist/DJ Carita: 13520 Les Baux-de-Provence
Tel: 33(0)4 90 54 40 26   Fax: 33(0)4 90 92 63 04
brunogeddadj@aol.com

The Provençal Garden

The rose of grasse: fragrances and flavors

Musée International de la Parfumerie /
International Museum of Perfume
8, place du Cours, 06130 Grasse
Tel: 33 (0)4 93 36 80 20   Fax: 33 (0)4 93 36 44 73
www.museesdegrasse.com / info@museesdegrasse.com

Prieuré de Salagon
Musée-Conservatoire ethnologique de Haute-Provence /
Ethnologic Museum and Conservatory of Haute-Provence
04300 Mane,   Tel: 33(0)4 92 75 70 50   Fax: 33 (0)4 92 75 70 58
www.musee-de-salagon.com / info@musee-de-salagon.com

Château Val Joanis: 84120 Pertuis
Tel: 33 (0)4 90 79 20 77   Fax: 33 (0)4 90 09 69 52
www.val-joanis.com / info.visites@val-joanis.com

Mad about figs

Pierre Baud
Pépinières Baud : Le Palis, 84110 Vaison-La-Romaine
Tel: 33(0)4 90 36 08 46   Fax: 33(0)4 90 28 71 25
pepinieres@fig-baud.com

Francis et Jacqueline Honoré
Les Figuières, Mas de Luquet,
13690 Graveson
Tel: 33(0)4 90 95 72 03   Fax: 33(0)4 90 95 76 23
www.lesfiguieres.com / info@lesfiguieres.com

Flavors and Health

Savoring gold - the menton lemon

Office de Tourisme / Tourist Office
Palais de l'Europe: 8, avenue Boyer, 06500 Menton
Tel: 33(0)4 92 41 76 76   Fax: 33(0)4 92 41 76 78
www.ville-menton.fr / tourisme@menton.fr

Philippe Rigollot
Service des jardins / Garden Services
Mairie de Menton, 17, rue de la République, 06500 Menton
Tel: 33(0)4 93 35 32 18   Fax: 33(0)4 93 41 49 43
mairie@ville-menton.fr

Foundation Escoffier
3, rue Auguste-Escoffier, 06270 Villeneuve-Loubet
Tel: 33(0)4 93 20 80 51   Fax: 33(0)4 93 73 93 79
www.foundation-escoffier.org / contact@foundation-escoffier.org

The tasteful vegetables of the Var

Daniel and Denise Vuillon
Le jardin des Olivades: 257 Chemin de la Petite-Garenne
83190 Ollioules,   Tel/Fax: 33(0)4 94 30 03
13www.olivades.com / vuillon@olivades.com

Moulin à Huile Baussy
Gérard Baussy et fils: rue Bourboutel, 06530 Spéracèdes
Tel: 33(0)4 93 60 58 59   Fax: 33 (0)493 60 62 58
www.moulinbaussy.com

Family cuisine

Monique Caulet
Les amis de la cuisine provençale / Friends of Provençal cuisine/
Espace Jean-Baptiste Reboul
Chemin des Aires, 83136, La Roquebrussane
Tel: 33(0)4 94 86 93 36   Fax: 33(0)4 94 86 80 29

Myriam Desestres
38, traverse Parangon, 13008 Marseille
Tel: 33(0)4 91 25 08 48   Specialist in the art of simplicity

Guy and Paula Chauvin
Association Accueil en Provence / Welcome to Provence Association
La Campagne Gerbaud, 84160 Lourmarin
Tel: 33(0)4 90 68 11 83   Fax: 33(0)4 90 68 37 12
cgerbaud@aol.com / www.lourmarin.com/gerbaud

Jean-Marc Biojoux
Directeur développement tourisme et commerce
Chambre de commerce et d'industrie du pays d'Arles /
Director - Development of tourism and commerce
Chamber of Commerce and Industry of Arles
Avenue Division France Libre, 13200 Arles
Tel: 33 (0)4 90 99 08 08f   Fax: 33(0)4 90 99 08 00
www.arles.cci.fr / jmbiojoux@arles.cci.fr

Jeanne Dulac
Ecole du goût et de l'olive : Domaine de Rousty /
School of Taste and the Olive
13103 Max-Blanc-des-Alpilles,   Tel/Fax: 33(0)4 90 49 10 68

Soraya and Patrick Lagarrigue
La Route des Epices / The Spice Route: 32, rue de la Calèche, 34170
Castelnau-le-Lez,   Tel/Fax: 33(0)4 67 02 26 12
www.route-epices.com / lagarrigue.patrick@free.fr

Voyage and Discovery

Les Jardins de l'Alchimiste / The Alchemist's Garden
Mas de la Brune, 13810 Eygalières
Tel: 33 (0)4 90 90 67 77   Fax: 33 (0)4 90 95 99 21
www.jardin-alchimiste.com / contact@jardin-alchimiste.com

Michel Santinelli
Syndicat des producteurs de truffes noires des Alpes-Maritimes/
Association of black truffle producers of the Alpes-Maritimes
58 MIN Fleurs 6, 06296 Nice Cedex 3
Tel: 33(0)4 97 35 76 40   Fax: 33(0)4 97 25 76 59
fdgeda@atsat.com

Painter's gardens

Office de Tourisme / Tourist Office
Boulevard des Lices, 13200 Arles
Tel: 33(0)4 90 18 41 20   Fax: 33(0)4 90 18 41 29
Circuit "Sur les pas de Vincent Van Gogh" tous les samedis à 14h30
en francais et en anglais
Guided Tour "In the footsteps of Vincent Van Gogh" Saturdays at
2:30pm, in French and English
www.tourisme.ville-arles.fr / ot-arles@visitprovence.com

Office de Tourisme / Tourist Office
Place Jean-Jaurès, 13210 Saint-Rémy-de-Provence
Tel: 33(0)4 90 92 05 22   Fax: 33(0)4 90 92 38 52
www.saintremy-de-provence.com
tourisme.st.remy@wanadoo.fr

Atelier Paul Cézanne / Paul Cézanne's Studio
9, avenue Paul-Cézanne, 13090 Aix-en-Provence
Tel: 33(0)4 42 21 06 53   Fax: 33(0)4 42 21 90 34
www.atelier-cezanne.com / info@atelier-cezanne.com

Musée Renoir / Renoir Museum
Chemin des Collettes, 06800 Cagnes-sur-Mer
Tel: 33(0)4 93 20 61 07   Fax: 33(0)4 93 73 09 20
Conservateur / Curator: Frédérique Verlinden
www.cagnes-tourisme.com/renoir

Flower waters and essences

Albert Vieille SA Matieres Premieres Aromatiques
629 Route de grasse, 06220 Vallauris
Tel: 33(0)4 93 64 16 72   Fax: 33(0)4 93 64 80 07
www.albertvieille.com / info@albertvieille.com
(Wholesale sales)

Ets Lavoillotte Solubarôme
1486 Chemin de la Plaine, 06250 Mougins
Tel/Fax: 33(0)4 93 75 03 68
solubarome.free.fr / solubarôme@hotmail.com
(Retail sales)

Mémoire de Garrigue
BP7 30210 Vers-pont-du-gard, Route du pont-du-gard
30210 Vers-Pont-du-Gard
Tel : 0 820 903 330 Fax : 33(0)4 66 37 51 50
contact@pontdugard.fr/www.pontdugard.fr

BIBLIOGRAPHY

L'Âge d'or de la parfumerie à Grasse, d'après les archives CHIRIS, 1768-1967, Édisud, 1987.

ARON, Jean-Paul, *Le Mangeur du XIXᵉ siècle*, Payot, 1989.

BARBIER, Élisabeth, *Les Gens de Mogador*, Pocket, 2004.

BENOIT, Fernand, *La Provence et le Comtat venaissin: arts et traditions populaires*, Aubanel, 1975.

BERNARD, Émile, *Conversations avec Cézanne*, édition critique présentée par P.M. Doran, Macula, 1978.

BIEHN, Michel, *Couleurs de Provence*, Flammarion, 2000.

CACHIN, Françoise, « C'est l'Éden retrouvé » dans *Méditerranée: De Courbet à Matisse*, Réunion des musées nationaux, 2000.

CHANOT-BULLIER, C., *Vieii Receto de Cousino Prouvençalo / Vieilles Recettes de cuisine provençale*, Tacussel, 1976.

CHIBOIS, Jacques, et BAUSSAN, Olivier, *Saveurs et parfums de l'huile d'olive*, Flammarion, 1999.

COLETTE, *Prisons et paradis*, Fayard, 1986.

CURNONSKY, *Recettes des provinces de France*, Les Productions de Paris, 1962.

DAVID, Elizabeth, « Foods of Legend » dans *An Omelette and a Glass of Wine*, Penguin, 1984.

DURRELL, Lawrence, *Quinte ou la version Landru*, traduit de l'anglais par Paule Guivarch, Gallimard, 1986.

ESCOFFIER, Auguste, *Souvenirs inédits*, Jeanne Laffitte, 1985.

FELL, Derek, *Le Jardin de Renoir*, traduit de l'anglais par Sylvie Cohen, Robert Laffont, 1992.

FORTESCUE, Winifred, *Perfume from Provence*, Hearst Books, 1993.

FUSTIER-DAUTIER, Nerte, *Les Bastides de Provence et leur jardins*, Serg, 1977, Bastides et jardins, Parenthèses, 1996.

GAUDENZI, Jean-Louis de., *La Cuisine de Nostradamus*, Multitudes, 2000.

Grimod de La Reynière, Alexandre Balthazar, « Almanach des gourmands », dans *Écrits gastronomiques*, 10-18, 1997.

JOUVEAU, René, *La Cuisine provençale de tradition populaire*, Imprimerie Bene, 1976.

KURLANSKY, Mark, *Cod: A Biography of the Fish that Changed the World*, Vintage, 1999.

LA QUINTINIE, Jean-Baptiste de., *Instruction pour les jardins fruitiers et potagers*, Actes Sud, 2003.

LIEUTAGHI, Pierre, *Jardin des savoirs, jardin d'histoire*, Les Alpes de lumière, n.d.

LIEUTAGHI, Pierre, « Le Recours à la terre » dans *Le Sauvage: Le Nouvel Observateur: Le Jardin: Modèle de Gestion du Monde*, été 1980, nº 71.

MADOX, Ford, *Provence*, The Ecco Press, 1979.

MARTIN-VILLEVIEILLE, Simone, *Histoire des recettes de Provence*, Jeanne Laffitte, 2000.

MAUPASSANT, Guy de., *Sur l'eau*. Pocket, 1999.

MAURIÈRES, Arnaud, OSSART, Éric, *Jardiniers de paradis*, Le Chêne, 2000.

MIKANOWSKI, Lindsay et Patrick. *Tomate*, Le Chêne, 1999.

MISTRAL, Frédéric, *Dernière prose d'Almanach*, traduit de l'occitan par Pierre Devoluy, Bernard Grasset, 1930.

MISTRAL, Frédéric, *Mes origines. Mémoires et récits*, Aubéron, 2004.

PAGNOL, Marcel, *La Gloire de mon père*, De Fallois, 1997.

PAPANAK, Victor, *The Green Imperative: Ecology and Ethics in Design and Architecture*, Thames and Hudson, 1995.

PAPON, abbé Jean-Pierre, *Voyage de Provence*, La Découverte, 1984.

PICKVANCE, Roland, *Van Gogh in Arles*. The Metropolitan Museum of Art / Harry N. Abrams, 1984.

PONGE, Francis, *Comment une figue de paroles et pourquoi*, présentation par Jean-Marie Gleize, Flammarion, 1997.

RACINE, Michel, BOURSIER-MOUGENOT, Ernest. *Jardins de la côte d'Azur*, Édisud, 1987.

Recettes en Provence paysanne (collectif), CETA « Accueil en Provence paysanne », n.d.

RIGOLLOT, Philippe, « Le citron de Menton », *Hommes et plantes*, nº 37, printemps 2001.

Rose, Rosa, Rosae, Musée international de la Parfumerie, 1991.

SERGUIER, Clément, *Pour un panier de figues*. Barthélemy, 1992.

SERRES, Olivier de., *Le Théâtre d'agriculture et mesnage des champs*, introduction de Pierre Lieutaghi, Actes Sud, 2001.

SMOLLETT, Tobias George, *Voyages à travers la France et l'Italie*, extraits traduits de l'anglais par André Fayot, José Corti, 1994.

STENDHAL, *Voyage dans le Midi*, Maspero, 1984.

VAN GOGH, Vincent, *Lettres à son frère Théo*, Grasset, 2002.

ACKNOWLEDGMENTS

I would first like to thank Jacques Chibois for his immense talent and his constant generosity. I also appreciate his humor, kindness, intuition, love for his work, and even his mystery. I also wish to thank all those who welcomed me so warmly into their homes and workplaces and made this book possible. The publishing team at Aubanel was constantly patient, and my husband shared, as always, all the ups and downs of book production. Thanks also to the team at Stewart, Tabori & Chang. And finally, to American chef Dan Barber of Stone Barns, for his participation in a joint effort on both continents to keep the world from leaving the earth behind.

Louisa Jones

Guy Hervais would like to thank the following for their fine taste and their cooperation:

Bernadette Lassalette, Villa Saint-Louis, bed and breakfast, Lourmarin
Tel: 33(0)4 90 68 39 18.
Artichaut, Linens and objects for the home, Lourmarin
Tel: 33(0)4 90 68 03 08.
Le thé dans l'encrier, Tea Salon and Library, Lourmarin
Tel: 33(0)4 90 68 88 41.
Françoise Fabre, Fragonard, Grasse.
Florence Geslin, S.A. Albert Vieille, Vallauris.
Philippe Rigollot, Espaces verts, Menton
Frédéric Ratto, La Bastide de Galon - Oil Mill, Cucuron.
Tel: 33(0)4 90 08 90 01.
Mme & M. Honoré, fig producers, Graveson.
Mme & M. Vuillon, vegetable and tomato producers, Olioules.
Edith Mézard, Château de l'Ange, Lumières.
Michel Biehn, for his provençal fabrics, L'Isle-sur-la-Sorgue.
Musée Marc Deydier, Cucuron.
Tel: 33(0)4 90 77 28 37.
La Cuisine à Simone, ustensiles culinaires, Lourmarin
Tel: 33(0)4 90 68 39 10.
Michel Canavese, an itinerant fishmonger of exceptional quality.

And Bibi, for a certain propensity for happiness

ACKNOWLEDGMENTS

I would first like to thank Jacques Chibois for his immense talent and his constant generosity. I also appreciate his humor, kindness, intuition, love for his work, and even his mystery. I also wish to thank all those who welcomed me so warmly into their homes and workplaces and made this book possible. The publishing team at Aubanel was constantly patient, and my husband shared, as always, all the ups and downs of book production. Thanks also to the team at Stewart, Tabori & Chang. And finally, to American chef Dan Barber of Stone Barns, for his participation in a joint effort on both continents to keep the world from leaving the earth behind.

Louisa Jones

Guy Hervais would like to thank the following for their fine taste and their cooperation:

Bernadette Lassalette, Villa Saint-Louis, bed and breakfast, Lourmarin
Tel: 33(0)4 90 68 39 18.
Artichaut, Linens and objects for the home, Lourmarin
Tel: 33(0)4 90 68 03 08.
Le thé dans l'encrier, Tea Salon and Library, Lourmarin
Tel: 33(0)4 90 68 88 41.
Françoise Fabre, Fragonard, Grasse.
Florence Geslin, S.A. Albert Vieille, Vallauris.
Philippe Rigollot, Espaces verts, Menton
Frédéric Ratto, La Bastide de Galon - Oil Mill, Cucuron.
Tel: 33(0)4 90 08 90 01.
Mme & M. Honoré, fig producers, Graveson.
Mme & M. Vuillon, vegetable and tomato producers, Olioules.
Edith Mézard, Château de l'Ange, Lumières.
Michel Biehn, for his provençal fabrics, L'Isle-sur-la-Sorgue.
Musée Marc Deydier, Cucuron.
Tel: 33(0)4 90 77 28 37.
La Cuisine à Simone, ustensiles culinaires, Lourmarin
Tel: 33(0)4 90 68 39 10.
Michel Canavese, an itinerant fishmonger of exceptional quality.

And Bibi, for a certain propensity for happiness

PHOTO CREDITS

Graphic design:
SÉVERINE MORIZET